"Humility is seldom thought about in our Christian community. In his masterful way, C. J. Mahaney gives us a much-needed wake-up call on this important subject. I highly recommend this book."

JERRY BRIDGES
AUTHOR OF *THE PURSUIT OF HOLINESS*

"My friend C. J. Mahaney tackles a subject of immense importance. Since God opposes the proud and gives grace to the humble, what could be more important than understanding and developing true humility as a lightning rod for grace? C. J.'s book is biblical, honest, and full of helpful insights. We need less egomania and more humility and servanthood in our churches today. May God use this book to remind us that 'only the humble are sane.'"

RANDY ALCORN
AUTHOR OF *HEAVEN* AND *THE GRACE AND TRUTH PARADOX*

"We need to be reminded daily that God is opposed to the proud. We need to be told once again what greatness is in the eyes of God. This is important for leaders in the church, leaders in families, and for anyone who desires to live a life of excellence that is pleasing to Him. I am grateful for C. J. Mahaney's honest and accurate treatment of this 'accepted' sin. Let the truth that is explained in this book break you of pride and reap within you the pleasing aroma of humility. God not only is opposed to the proud, but He exalts the humble."

JOHN MACARTHUR
PASTOR AND TEACHER, GRACE COMMUNITY CHURCH

"C. J. Mahaney is not humble. At least, that's what he'll tell you. And that's one reason he's so well qualified to write this book. I've read it. I've seen humility in his life—and in the lives of those he's taught. If you're fighting pride—like I am—you should read it, too. And if you're not fighting pride, you really need to read it!"

MARK E. DEVER
SENIOR PASTOR, CAPITOL HILL BAPTIST CHURCH
AUTHOR, *NINE MARKS OF A HEALTHY CHURCH*

"This is the right book from the right man at the right time. More than any other man I have known, C. J. Mahaney has taught me what humility really is. This is a man whose humility is a gift to the entire church. He knows that humility is strength, and that God uses the humble in a powerful way. He understands the danger of pride and calls us all to aspire to a legacy of greatness—a greatness that shows the entire world the glory of God. He points us to a cross-centered worldview that will transform every dimension of life."

"A wonderful, sobering, humbling, God-centered, Bible-based book on humility by an author who truly exemplifies it in his own life. I especially appreciated Mahaney's suggestions for practical disciplines to help us cultivate humility before God. This message will tend to keep us and our churches from self-destruction due to pride, will make us thankful for little blessings in everyday life, and will bring us closer to God."

"In *Humility: True Greatness*, C. J. Mahaney provides a clear and helpful battlefield manual for the believer's ongoing growth, the fight against pride, and the cultivation of humility. C. J. is no dry-land sailor in this conflict. He and his dear congregation manifest the Spirit's sovereign grace-work in both their personal and corporate humility and in their seriousness about dealing with pride. A 'proud Christian' is an oxymoron. May the Lord of Glory, who humbled himself unto death, use this book to slay pride in you, and to form in you the true greatness of servanthood and self-denial."

HUMILITY:
TRUE GREATNESS

C. J. MAHANEY

Multnomah Books

HUMILITY: TRUE GREATNESS

published by Multnomah Books
© 2005 by Sovereign Grace Ministries
International Standard Book Number: 978-1-59052-326-1

Cover design by Studiogearbox.com
Cover image by Getty Images/Eric Tucker

Italics in Scripture quotations are the author's emphasis.
Unless otherwise indicated, Scripture quotations are from:
The Holy Bible, *English Standard Version* © 2001 by Crossway Bibles,
a division of Good News Publishers.
Used by permission. All rights reserved.
Other Scripture quotations are from:
The Holy Bible, New International Version (NIV)
© 1973, 1984 by International Bible Society,
used by permission of Zondervan Publishing House

Published in the United States by WaterBrook Multnomah, an imprint of the Crown
Publishing Group, a division of Random House Inc., New York.

MULTNOMAH and its mountain colophon are registered trademarks of Random House Inc.

For information:
MULTNOMAH BOOKS
12265 ORACLE BOULEVARD, SUITE 200
COLORADO SPRINGS, CO 80921

Library of Congress Cataloging-in-Publication Data
Mahaney, C. J.
 Humility : true greatness / C.J. Mahaney.
   p. cm.
 ISBN 1-59052-326-1
 1. Humility—Religious aspects—Christianity. I. Title.
 BV4647.H8M34 2005
 241'.4—dc22

                              2005020843

09 10—15 14 13 12

To my son, Chad.

CONTENTS

PART I
OUR GREATEST FRIEND, OUR GREATEST ENEMY
The Battle of Humility Versus Pride

PART II
THE GREAT REVERSAL
Our Savior and the Secret of True Greatness

FOREWORD

HUMILITY IS A FUNNY THING.

On the one hand, it's an extremely desirable trait. Most of us, as Christians, would say we want to be humble, right? Or at least we want to be *thought of* as humble. At the same time, few of us have given attention to what being humble actually means. Even fewer have considered what it takes to grow in humility.

In place of true humility we learn certain words or phrases that we believe make us sound humble: "Oh, really, it was nothing" or "Anyone could have done it." We cast our eyes down and shrug our shoulders or maybe even blush. Of course, we don't really mean it—inside we're congratulating ourselves for how humble we look and feel. We want that reputation but don't know how to get to the reality. Like children playing dress-up in their parents' clothes, we're only *acting* humble; none of it really fits us.

I'm glad you've been drawn to this book. I believe it can help you make humility more than just a performance. In these pages you'll learn how to make humility the everyday attire of your life.

The author, C. J. Mahaney, is a dear friend of mine, and I've spent a great deal of time with him. We've worked together, traveled together, even lived together. (I rented a room in the Mahaney basement for a year while I was single.) I tell you this to say that I can verify the authenticity of what C. J. writes. He has fought the battles of pride that we all face. He's a man who by God's grace has cultivated and pursued the brand of humility that matters most—the kind that defines a lifetime of walking with God.

For me, the best example of this kind of humility is the fact that, after twenty-seven years of serving as senior pastor of Covenant Life Church, he chose to pass this role on to me. I'm only thirty, while C. J. is fifty-one and, in my opinion, in the prime of his life and ministry. And yet he trained and mentored me, then joyfully allowed me to step into his place. Most young pastors have to start their own church to get the chance to lead so soon, since few older men are willing to give up or share a position of leadership. C. J. was not only willing to make this transition but planned it for years so that I'd be positioned for success.

Though I've just begun my ministry at Covenant Life, C. J.'s example has inspired me to look ahead to when I can make the same handoff to the next leader of our church. Who knows? That ten-year-old boy running down the church hallway might one day be sitting behind my desk. And when that day comes, I hope I'll have the same humility of heart that C. J. has shown me.

I plan to keep learning from C. J., and I know you'll learn from him as you read this book. What I love about *Humility: True Greatness* is that it takes our focus away from the human audience we're so often preoccupied with and reminds us of the one Observer, our only Sovereign and Savior, whose attention can be captured by a heart and life that displays genuine humility. I pray that, as you read, your desire for true greatness in God's eyes will increase and overflow in a life of true humility.

Joshua Harris

INTRODUCTION

Writing about humility is a humbling experience. Who wants to volunteer to write on *this* subject? Not me. There've been countless times while completing this book when I've been inspired to think, *You idiot! Why did you agree to do this?* And I could entertain you for hours relating the comments and facial expressions of those who discovered I was authoring a work with this title.

I understand their reaction. If I met someone presuming to have something to say about humility, automatically I'd think him unqualified to speak on the subject.

So let me make this clear at the outset: I'm a proud man pursuing humility by the grace of God. I don't write as an authority on humility; I write as a fellow pilgrim walking with you on the path set for us by our humble Savior. I can only address you with confidence in the great and gracious God who has promised to give grace to the humble (see James 4:6; 1 Peter 5:5). That promise forms the heart of this book. And that promise is for every one of us who turns from his or her sins and trusts in the Savior.

The structure of this book is simple and straightforward.

In the first part we'll learn that, no matter our age or vocation, humility is our greatest friend and pride our greatest enemy.

In part two we'll discover that genuine humility requires a radical redefinition of success. We'll learn from Jesus Christ as He teaches His disciples the nature of true greatness, and why this greatness is attainable only through His death on the cross for sinners like you and me.

Finally, in part three we'll get very practical. We'll examine how to cultivate humility and weaken pride each and every day.

I hope you'll take this journey with me. I can certainly think of many who would make better guides. But I *have* experienced the *promise* of humility. His promise is real. And it's for you.

OUR GREATEST FRIEND, OUR GREATEST ENEMY

*The Battle of Humility
Versus Pride*

THE PROMISE OF HUMILITY

I N A CULTURE that so often rewards the proud—a world quick to admire and applaud the prideful, a world eager to bestow the label "great" on these same individuals—humility occasionally attracts some surprising attention.

Take, for example, the bestselling book *Good to Great*. Since 2001, this leadership manual from Jim Collins has become one of the most popular and influential in the business world. I rarely meet a leader who hasn't read it. The book is driven by this question: Can a good company become a great company, and if so, how? To find the answer, Collins and a team of researchers spent five years studying eleven corporations that had made the leap from being merely *good* companies to being *great* ones.

I had the chance to hear Jim Collins speak on this

topic to an audience of pastors and business leaders. In his presentation, Collins identified two specific character qualities shared by the CEOs of these good-to-great companies.

The first was no surprise: These men and women possessed incredible professional will—they were driven, willing to endure anything to make their company a success.

But the second trait these leaders had in common wasn't something the researchers expected to find: These driven leaders were self-effacing and modest. They consistently pointed to the contribution of others and didn't like drawing attention to themselves. "The good-to-great leaders never wanted to become larger-than-life heroes," Collins writes. "They never aspired to be put on a pedestal or become unreachable icons. They were seemingly ordinary people quietly producing extraordinary results."

When Collins interviewed people who worked for these leaders, he says they "continually used words like *quiet, humble, modest, reserved, shy, gracious, mild-mannered, self-effacing, understated, did not believe his own clippings;* and so forth" to describe them.[1]

IN GOD'S GAZE

Here, it appears, is open acknowledgment of humility's value—recognition that humility *works*, that it goes far in building respect for those who have it and in inspiring trust and confidence from people around them.

Yes, amazingly, humility sometimes attracts the world's notice.

But here's something even more astonishing: Humility gets *God's* attention. In Isaiah 66:2 we read these words from the Lord:

This is the one *to whom I will look*:
he who is humble and contrite in spirit
and trembles at my word.

This profound passage points us to an altogether different motivation and purpose for humility than we will ever find in the pages of a secular business manual. Here we find motivation and purpose rooted in this amazing fact: *Humility draws the gaze of our Sovereign God.*

If we understand the background of this passage, we find even richer meaning. Here God is addressing the Israelites, a people with a unique identity. Chosen by God from among all the nations on earth, they possessed both the temple and the Torah—the Law of God. But they didn't tremble at His word. In a sense they had everything going for them except what was most important. They lacked humility before God.

So in this passage, God in His mercy is drawing the

Israelites' attention away from their prideful assumption of privilege as His chosen people and away from their preoccupation with the trappings of religion. These things don't attract His active and gracious gaze. But humility does.

GOD HELPS THOSE...

The eyes of God are a theme running throughout Scripture. Take, for example, the familiar words of 2 Chronicles 16:9, "For the eyes of the LORD run to and fro throughout the whole earth, to give strong support to those whose heart is blameless toward him." Obviously God doesn't have physical eyes; God is spirit (John 4:24). He doesn't need physical eyes, because He's also omniscient. Nothing escapes His notice. He's aware of all things.

But though He's aware of everything, He's also searching for something in particular, something that acts like a magnet to capture His attention and invite His active involvement. God is decisively drawn to humility. The person who is humble is the one who draws God's attention, and in this sense, drawing His attention means also attracting His grace—His unmerited kindness. Think about that: There's something you can do to attract more of God's gracious, undeserved, supernatural strength and assistance!

What a promise! Listen to this familiar passage again

for the very first time: "God...gives grace to the humble" (James 4:6). Contrary to popular and false belief, it's not "those who help themselves" whom God helps; it's those who *humble* themselves.

This is the promise of humility. God is personally and providentially supportive of the humble. And the grace He extends to the humble is indescribably rich. As Jonathan Edwards wrote, "The pleasures of humility are really the most refined, inward, and exquisite delights in the world."[2] This book's purpose is to help position you to receive and experience those exquisite pleasures.

WHAT IS HUMILITY?

For me, Jim Collins's book was an encouraging reminder that even in a world that celebrates the proud, humility is still valued. But books like *Good to Great* have severe limitations; they can take us only so far in understanding humility because they're not rooted in a biblical worldview. Our definition of humility must be biblical and not simply pragmatic, and in order to be biblical it must begin with God. As John Calvin wrote, "It is evident that man never attains to a true self-knowledge until he has previously contemplated the face of God, and come down after such contemplation to look into himself."[3]

That's where the following definition can help us:

Humility is honestly assessing ourselves in light of God's holiness and our sinfulness.

That's the twin reality that all genuine humility is rooted in: God's holiness and our sinfulness. Without an honest awareness of both these realities (and we'll reflect on both throughout this book), all self-evaluation will be skewed and we'll fail to either understand or practice true humility. We'll miss out on experiencing the promise and the pleasures that humility offers.

That's why I want to direct you to God's help for evaluating your life honestly, to understand whether you're growing in the humility that draws His gaze and attracts more of His grace.

DO YOU HAVE IT?

A few years ago our church—Covenant Life Church in Gaithersburg, Maryland—celebrated its twenty-fifth anniversary. As we gathered on this occasion to rejoice together, Gary Ricucci, who's part of our pastoral team and one of the church's founding pastors, stood before us to present an overview of our history. He observed that though much had changed over the previous twenty-five years—such as the physical appearance of certain pastors like myself—the particular values that were present at our church's inception had remained unchanged.

Listening intently to Gary that morning was a church member and small-group leader named Jim. Before attending Covenant Life, he'd been a part of a congregation where, regretfully, a serious church split had taken place. As he listened to Gary describe our church's enduring values, Jim's mind was busy comparing these with the values evident in his former church. "Why was my experience so different?" Jim wondered.

He heard Gary affirm that, right from the beginning, Covenant Life Church had a love for God's Word.

And Jim said to himself, *Yes, we had that.*

Gary continued, "We were in love with Jesus Christ and grateful for His substitutionary sacrifice on the cross."

Yes, Jim thought, *we had that, too.*

"We loved grace, and we loved worship."

Yep, had that.

"We believed in the importance of relationships," Gary added.

Once again Jim inwardly responded, *Okay, we had that.*

Then Gary said, "And there was a strong emphasis on humility, especially among the leaders."

And Jim thought, *Nope. That we did not have.*

Let's ask ourselves: When it comes to the values we live by, what will others say about us one day? Will they testify that *humility* characterized our lives?

So many human ventures, so many grand designs of mankind, have been undermined because humility was lacking on the part of those involved. In the following chapter we'll take a look at just how dangerous pride is, but our motivation for rooting out pride must go beyond a knowledge of its pitfalls and perils. Our pursuit should be driven by the amazing promise that humility holds out to us: *God gives grace to the humble!*

What are you building with your life? A marriage? A family? A business? A church? A career? In all your ventures, are you aware of your need for God's grace to give your efforts lasting value? Do you long for God's providential help and blessing? Then let's allow the promise of humility to shape our life and choices, so our children and others will one day look back and say of us, *They had that. They had humility. They had what mattered.*

Notes

1. Jim Collins, *Good to Great* (New York: Harper Collins, 2001), 27.
2. From the March 2, 1723, entry in Jonathan Edwards's diary, *Memoir of Jonathan Edwards,* http://www.tracts.ukgo.com/memoir_jonathan_edwards.pdf (accessed August 3, 2005).
3. John Calvin, *Institutes of the Christian Religion,* vol. 1 (Grand Rapids, MI: Wm. B. Eerdmans Publishing Company, 1990), 38.

2

THE PERILS OF PRIDE

Winston Churchill, who perfected the art of the clever put-down, once described a political opponent as "a modest little man who has a good deal to be modest about." The last part of his remark is an accurate description of me—though I can't say I'm humble, I certainly have much to be humble about! My general ineptness is well known to all who have even a casual acquaintance with me, and that's no exaggeration.

If you were to speak to any of my friends, they would confirm how I continually surprise them with fresh discoveries of my inadequacies. I even provide them a certain degree of entertainment, especially when it comes to the hands-on and the mechanical.

One day my daughter informed me that our car was making a strange noise, so I went out to investigate. She tried to prepare me, but in no way did I anticipate the violent shrieking that assaulted my ears upon starting the car. I immediately turned off the engine.

In such a moment, wisdom demands one course of action only: Get out of the car, walk back into the house, and call a trustworthy auto-repair service.

That would have been the appropriate and prudent response. Instead, I followed the arrogant male instinct, which requires at bare minimum that the male lift the hood and stare intently at the engine. After all, neighbors might be watching, and we want to at least give the appearance that we have *some* mechanical knowledge.

However, my world growing up was athletics, not automobiles. And to be honest, it's not just car engines that I'm inept with; it's the entire car. Lest you think I'm overstating it, let me briefly interrupt this account with another.

The following is a true story. Really.

NEEDING HELP

A while back, someone informed me that my car's rear left tire—or was it the rear right?—was low on air. Now, in fact, I had no idea how to put air in a car tire. So I turned to a friend—a *close* friend, I'll have you know—and asked for his help.

In such a moment, the godly and servant-hearted response from a friend would be to cheerfully answer, "Yes, let me help you." Instead, my good friend exclaimed, "I cannot believe it. I *cannot* believe it! *You* don't know how to put *air* in your *tire?*"

On and on like this he went, until he faced me squarely and added, "You, my friend, are a moron."

My friend was merely having fun at my expense, but the truth of the matter is that on a previous occasion I had actually tried, on my own, to put air in my car's tire. As I knelt to place the air hose on the stem—or whatever that little dealy's called where you attach the hose to the tire—the extremely loud noise that erupted was an intimidating *PHHHHT! PHHHHHHT!*

Then a loud ringing started: *DING DING DING DING!* I was suddenly consumed by an intense fear that my tire was only seconds from blowing up. *It's going to explode,* I told myself, *and you're going to die. And at your funeral, all your friends—while wiping away tears in the midst of their mourning—will be shaking their heads and saying to themselves, "What an idiot!"*

I'm convinced that the sum effect of my attempt that day was only to let out more air than I put in. And as I drove away from the station with a badly underinflated tire, I could almost hear the faint sound of the station attendant's laughter following me home.

AGAINST ALL LOGIC

So, given my personal history, what groundless self-assurance could possibly motivate me to lift the hood that day to examine my engine? The only thing I actually know how to do is check whether the container for window-washer fluid needs refilling. So I checked that—with great authority. (It was more than half full.)

Then I shut the hood (also with great authority) and, proud fool that I am, got back into the car and turned the ignition once more—as if my having merely stared at the engine was sufficient to repair it; as if the broken parts were now calling to one another, "He's seen us! Get back together, quick!"

Yet as I turned the key again, the same violent shriek issued forth.

Only at this point did I finally go back in the house to do what I should have done earlier: I telephoned the repair shop to notify them of my car's condition—fully ready to pass along to them my firm conviction that the problem was *not* the window-washer fluid container.

Now you might assume that in a normal human being, such ineptness couldn't possibly coexist with any significant measure of pride. Someone as unskilled as I am would, naturally, be humble, right? However, without a doubt I can assure you that both incompetence and pride are very evident in my life. In fact, we'll discover in this book how pride seems to have a strange and sure way of ignoring logic altogether. Can you relate?

The sad fact is that none of us are immune to the logic-defying, blinding effects of pride. Though it shows up in different forms and to differing degrees, it infects us all. The real issue here is not *if* pride exists in your heart; it's *where* pride exists and *how* pride is being expressed in your life. Scripture shows us that pride is strongly and dangerously rooted in all our lives, far more than most of us care to admit or even think about.

John Stott has clearly thought about this and wrote the following: "At every stage of our Christian development and in every sphere of our Christian discipleship, pride is the greatest enemy and humility our greatest friend."[1]

We've seen promise of humility—the gracious support of God. But we must also be aware of the great perils of pride—not just occasionally or under certain circumstances, but at *every* stage and in *every* sphere. Throughout our time on this earth, and in every arena of our lives, you and I share a common greatest enemy: pride.

THE FIRST SIN

Pride has quite the history, one that precedes Adam and Eve.

Pride, it seems, was the very first sin. Isaiah 14 records

the downfall of a king, but not a mere earthly ruler. This king is the embodiment of God-defying arrogance, but the language used here apparently references the rebellion and fall of Satan himself.

In Isaiah 14:13, the motivation behind Satan's rebellion is exposed: "You said in your heart, 'I will ascend to heaven; above the stars of God I will set my throne on high.'" Led by the prideful Lucifer, powerful angelic creatures possessing beauty and glory far beyond our comprehension arrogantly desired recognition and status equal to God Himself. In response, God swiftly and severely judged them.

Pride not only appears to be the earliest sin, but it is at the core of all sin. "Pride," John Stott writes, "is more than the first of the seven deadly sins; it is itself the essence of all sin."[2]

Indeed, from God's perspective, pride seems to be *the* most serious sin. From my study, I'm convinced there's nothing God hates more than this. God righteously hates all sin, of course, but biblical evidence abounds for the conclusion that there's no sin more offensive to Him than pride.

When His Word reveals those things "that the LORD hates" and "that are an abomination to him," it's the proud man's "haughty eyes" that head up the list (Proverbs 6:16–17).

When the personified wisdom of God speaks out, these clear words are emphasized: "I hate pride and arrogance" (Proverbs 8:13, NIV).

And consider the divine perspective on pride revealed in Proverbs 16:5: "Everyone who is arrogant in heart is an abomination to the LORD; be assured, he will not go unpunished."

Stronger language for sin simply cannot be found in Scripture.

CONTENDING WITH GOD

Why does God hate pride so passionately?

Here's why: *Pride is when sinful human beings aspire to the status and position of God and refuse to acknowledge their dependence upon Him.*

Charles Bridges once noted how pride lifts up one's heart against God and "contends for supremacy" with Him. That's a keenly insightful and biblical definition of pride's essence: contending for supremacy with God, and lifting up our hearts against Him.

For purposes of personal confession, I began adopting this definition of pride a few years ago after I came to realize that, to some degree, I'd grown unaffected by pride in my life. Though I was still confessing pride, I knew I wasn't sufficiently convicted of it. So rather than just confessing to God that "I was proud in that situation" and appealing for His forgiveness, I learned to say instead, "Lord, in that moment, with that attitude and that action, *I was contending for supremacy with You.* That's what it was all about. Forgive me."

And rather than confessing to another person, "That statement was prideful on my part; will you please forgive me?" I began saying, "What I just did was contending for supremacy with God," and only then asking for the person's forgiveness. This practice increased a weight of conviction in my heart about the seriousness of this sin.

Pride takes innumerable forms but has only one end: self-glorification. That's the motive and ultimate purpose of pride—to rob God of legitimate glory and to pursue self-glorification, contending for supremacy with Him. The proud person seeks to glorify himself and not God, thereby attempting in effect to deprive God of something only He is worthy to receive.

No wonder God opposes pride. No wonder He *hates* pride. Let that truth sink into your thinking.

GOD'S ACTIVE OPPOSITION TO PRIDE

Now let me ask you: What do *you* hate?

I'll tell you what I hate. I've got two lists. One is a silly list that begins with foods that I sometimes think must be products of the Fall. I detest meat loaf. I loathe sauerkraut. And I hate cottage cheese. I even hate it when anyone eats cottage cheese in my presence; it ruins my appetite.

I also despise any and all professional sports teams from New York City—that's simply part of my heritage, being born and raised in the Washington DC area.

That's just the beginning, a little sampling of my silly list of things I hate. But I also have a serious list of things I hate. I'm sure you have one, too.

I hate abortion.

I hate child abuse.

I hate racism.

What do you hate?

You and I hate nothing to the degree that God hates pride. His hatred for pride is pure, and His hatred is holy.

John Calvin wrote, "God cannot bear with seeing his glory appropriated by the creature in even the smallest degree, so intolerable to him is the sacrilegious arrogance of those who, by praising themselves, obscure his glory as far as they can."[3]

And because God cannot bear with this arrogance, He reveals Himself in Scripture as actively opposed to pride. *Actively.*

"God opposes the proud" (James 4:6; 1 Peter 5:5). "Opposes" in this statement is an active, present-tense verb, showing us that God's opposition to pride is an immediate and constant activity. The proud will not indefinitely escape discipline.

PRIDE'S POTENCY

To understand more of God's perspective on pride, we would do well to note its peculiarly destructive power. Jonathan Edwards called pride "the worst viper that is in the heart" and "the greatest disturber of the soul's peace and sweet communion with Christ"; he ranked pride as the most difficult sin to root out, and "the most hidden, secret and deceitful of all lusts."[4]

Despite this thorough understanding of its ugliness, Edwards himself constantly battled his own pride (a fact which gives me hope, knowing I'm not alone in this struggle). "What a foolish, silly, miserable, blind, deceived poor worm am I, when pride works," Edwards once wrote.[5] In his sermons and in his vast writings he constantly warned against pride, especially spiritual pride, which he viewed as the greatest cause of the premature ending of the Great Awakening, the revival that had brought so much spiritual vitality to the church in Edwards's day.

Pride also undermines unity and can ultimately divide a church. Show me a church where there's division, where there's quarreling, and I'll show you a church where there's pride.

Pride also brings down leaders. "Pride ruins pastors and churches more than any other thing," Mike Renihan has written. "It is more insidious in the church than radon in the home."[6] When you read about the next public figure to fall, remember Proverbs 16:18—"Pride goes before destruction, and a haughty spirit before a fall." That person's situation might appear circumstantially complicated, but at root it's not complicated: Pride goes before a fall.

GOD'S MERCIFUL WARNINGS

The warnings from Scripture about pride could not be more serious and sobering. And they're an expression of God's mercy, intended for our good.

God is merciful to warn us in this way. He's merciful in this act of revealing this sin to our hearts and in identifying its seriousness and potential consequences. He is merciful, and He intends to protect us. So throughout His Word, God exposes pride as our greatest enemy.

By unmasking pride—as well as introducing us to humility, our greatest friend—God is laying out for us the path to true greatness, a path that we will see most clearly in our Savior's life and death. Let's together begin walking that path in the next chapter.

Notes

1. John Stott, "Pride, Humility & God," *Sovereign Grace Online,* September/October 2000, http://www.sovereigngraceministries.org/sgo/v18no5/prt_pride.html (accessed August 3, 2005).

2. Ibid.

3. Commentary on Psalm 9:1–3 in John Calvin, *Commentary on the Book of Psalms*, trans. James Anderson (Grand Rapids, MI: Eerdmans, 1963), n.p.

4. Jonathan Edwards, *Advice to Young Converts* (Hartford Evangelical Tract Society, 1821), originating as a letter to Deborah Hatheway dated June 3, 1741.

5. From the March 2, 1723, entry in Jonathan Edwards's diary, *Memoir of Jonathan Edwards,* http://www.tracts.ukgo.com/memoir_jonathan_edwards.pdf (accessed August 3, 2005).

6. Mike Renihan, "A Pastor's Pride and Joy," *Tabletalk,* July 1999.

PART II

THE GREAT REVERSAL

*Our Savior and the Secret
of True Greatness*

3

GREATNESS REDEFINED

CHARLES SPURGEON once preached on the foolish-
ness of pride, calling it "a groundless thing" and "a
brainless thing" as well as "the maddest thing that can
exist."[1]

But despite the sheer folly and unreasonableness of
pride, it manifests its stubborn presence in countless ways
within all of us. Even the disciples of Jesus weren't
immune; in fact, they were prime offenders.

WHO'S THE GREATEST?

Pride was especially evident in the disciples' documented
pursuit of personal greatness and recognition. This pursuit
wasn't subtle, and it doesn't appear to be occasional. By
their own accounts, it was pronounced and apparently
continuous.

Notice, for example, what we learn in Mark 9 when the disciples and Jesus were traveling together. "They came to Capernaum. When he was in the house, he asked them, 'What were you arguing about on the road?'" (Mark 9:33, NIV).

But the disciples "kept silent"—no doubt from embarrassment and shame, "for on the way they had argued with one another about who was the greatest" (v. 34). Men who were receiving intensive training from Jesus Christ, the ultimate example of humility and servanthood, were embroiled in a full-scale dispute about their relative superiority to each other.

Jesus knew their hearts, just as He knows ours. So He immediately and insightfully addressed their selfish ambition: "And he sat down and called the twelve. And he said to them, 'If anyone would be first, he must be last of all and servant of all'" (Mark 9:35).

Jesus was radically redefining greatness. But His point apparently didn't sink in.

A BOLD QUESTION

In Mark 10 we find the brothers James and John approaching the Savior apart from their fellow disciples. In apparent agreement with each other about their own greatness, these two brothers bring to Jesus a special request.

Apparently John and James think the Savior shares their lofty assessment of themselves, because there's absolutely no lack of confidence evident in what they ask. "Teacher," they say to Him, "we want you to do for us whatever we ask of you." Jesus asks them what they desire. They answer, "Grant us to sit, one at your right hand and one at your left, in your glory" (Mark 10:35–37).

Mark has already informed us that Jesus and His disciples are going up to Jerusalem, where James and John and the others expect the Savior to immediately establish His kingdom, militarily and politically. He will thus enter His "glory" and the two brothers want a prominent place in it. They undoubtedly assumed such a prominent place for them is appropriate in light of their obvious superiority. "Let's settle this greatness issue *now*," they seem to be saying. "Who's the greatest? *We* are the greatest! And Master, we want You to acknowledge this fact by letting us sit on Your right and on Your left."

The prideful desires of their hearts are on full display. There's nothing subtle about their request. They're not asking for faith to endure His suffering. They're not asking for the privilege of supporting Him in and through His suffering. They want to be famous, pure and simple. James and John have defined greatness as position and power, and they want the title. They want the respect, the acclaim, and the importance. In their pride-dominated hearts, Jesus is just a means to their end of personal exaltation.

This passage by no means exonerates the other disciples, because sadly, the ten are no different. They somehow learn of James and John's request and become "indignant at James and John" (v. 41), revealing the presence in their own hearts not only of selfish ambition but also of self-righteousness.

Can you see yourself in this story? It's easy for us at times to disdain the disciples and fail to recognize our face in their portrait. They argued on the road about who was the greatest; we may not openly argue about this, but don't we engage in the same debate every day in our private thoughts? If you're like me, you compare yourself to others and look for opportunities to claim greater importance than them, just as the disciples did.

REDEFINITION

Thankfully, Jesus is merciful and gentle with our pride-drenched hearts, just as He was with His errant apostles. We read in Mark 10:42, "And Jesus called them to him." Can you sense the Savior's patience with them, as well as His loving commitment to teach them what they so desperately need to learn?

He reminds them first of what they've all observed during the long years of Roman occupation: "You know that those who are considered rulers of the Gentiles lord it over them, and their great ones exercise authority over them." Then the Savior sets down a contrast: "But it shall not be so among you."

What I find especially fascinating and instructive in His next words is that Jesus does *not* categorically criticize or forbid the desire and ambition to be great. Instead, He clearly redirects that ambition, redefines it, and purifies it: "But whoever would be great among you *must* be your servant, and whoever would be first among you *must* be slave of all" (vv. 43–44).

We always want to pay careful attention when that word *must* appears in Scripture. "Must" points us to something that's required, something that's indispensable. "You want to be great?" Jesus is saying. "Well, here's what has to happen. What's required is that you become a servant to others; it means nothing less than becoming the slave of everyone."

Remember that the Person standing there and making this statement is the ultimate example of true greatness Himself. And this is exactly what Jesus goes on to make clear: "For even the Son of Man came not to be served but to serve, and to give his life as a ransom for many" (v. 45).

In his excellent commentary on this passage, William Lane notes that Jesus is referring to "the reversal of all human ideas of greatness and rank."[2] A profound and historic reversal is taking place here—one that has to occur in each of our lives if we're to have any possibility of becoming truly great in God's eyes. It means turning upside down our entrenched, worldly ideas on the definition of greatness.

ALL AROUND US

The difference couldn't be more stark.

As sinfully and culturally defined, pursuing greatness looks like this: Individuals motivated by self-interest, self-indulgence, and a false sense of self-sufficiency pursue selfish ambition for the purpose of self-glorification.

Contrast that with the pursuit of true greatness as biblically defined: *Serving others for the glory of God.* This is the genuine expression of humility; this is true greatness as the Savior defined it.

Have you seen any examples of true greatness recently? The following are just a sampling from my observation and experience.

It's Bryce, the godly teenage son, who honors his parents and cares for his younger siblings—including his brother Eric, who suffers from autism.

It's Theresa, a single woman with an infectious laugh who cheerfully serves numerous families in our church.

It's Trey, a pastor-friend of mine who serves as an *assistant* pastor to his son Rich.

It's Eric, the successful businessman who volunteers each Sunday at our church, parking cars.

It's my daughter Kristin, who works tirelessly in her home to care for her husband, Brian, and her three small boys.

It's Dick, the single man and postal worker who lived a simple life so he could give generously to families who wanted to adopt children.

It's Ken, the father who left his job and all that was familiar to move his family across the country to a stronger local church.

And it's Bernie and Pearl, the couple in their eighties who, despite severe health issues, poured their hearts and lives into the small group that Bernie led. They are rejoicing with our Savior now.

True greatness is all around us. The question is, do we see it? Or more important, are we pursuing it? These examples and a thousand others are what it means to be great in the eyes of God—humbly serving others for His glory.

So we have two opposing definitions: greatness as sinfully and culturally defined versus greatness as biblically defined. The conflict between them continues to this day. The battle rages in our very hearts. We desperately need to be liberated. And it is the promise of freedom from pride that Jesus holds out to us.

Notes

1. Charles Haddon Spurgeon, "Pride and Humility," a sermon given August 17, 1856, in Southwark, England. http://christianunplugged.com/humility_3.htm (accessed August 3, 2005).
2. William L. Lane, *The Gospel of Mark*, The New International Commentary on the New Testament (Grand Rapids, MI: Eerdmans, 1974), 383.

GREATNESS
DEMONSTRATED

NOW WE REACH the crucial point. It's no exaggeration to say that understanding this chapter's content is essential to grasping the truth of this entire book. So if necessary, read slowly—because we are approaching holy ground.

Here's an essential truth: To learn true humility, we need more than a redefinition of greatness; we need even more than Jesus' personal example of humble service. *What we need is His death.*

Listen again to what Jesus said in Mark 10:45: "For even the Son of Man came not to be served but to serve, and to give his life as a ransom for many." The Savior here is clarifying for His disciples the *difference* between His example and theirs; He's emphasizing the uniqueness of His own sacrifice. He's telling them not only that true greatness is attained by emulating His example, but also that true greatness is not even possible for us apart from the Savior's unique sacrifice.

Jesus alone came to give His life as a ransom for the sins of many—and this separates Him from any other sacrificial service that anyone else anywhere could ever offer. Here we find what is completely, utterly, and categorically unique about the Savior and His example. And in true humility, our own service to others is always both an *effect* of His unique sacrifice and the *evidence* of it. His sacrifice alone makes it possible for us to achieve and experience true greatness in God's eyes.

Donald English expresses the point this way: "At the source of all Christian service in the world is the crucified and risen Lord who died to liberate us into such service."[1] That's why all Christian service not only reflects the Savior's example, but should also remind us of His sacrifice. Ultimately our Christian service exists only to draw attention to *this* source—to our crucified and risen Lord who gave Himself as a ransom for us all.

Let's move in for a closer look at this incomparable sacrifice.

JESUS LEADING THE WAY

In Mark 10 we find Jesus and His disciples on the road, going up to Jerusalem. This is the last journey of Jesus' ministry, and the final destination is in full view. The hour for which He ultimately came now approaches. The cross is on the horizon.

This long journey to Jerusalem and the cross will apparently be a lonely one for the Savior, for He's making it without the full understanding and support of His disciples. They continue to be blinded by selfish ambition, so He must continue to teach and instruct them and confront their arrogance.

And yet, however grieved His heart must surely be at this moment, we see Him "walking ahead of them" (v. 32). No one is prodding Him on; no one is forcing Him. He's *leading the way.* And the One leading the way is the *only* One in this group of travelers who's aware of what indescribable anguish awaits Him there.

Pause, if you will, and picture Him in your mind. Behold this lone figure out in front, fully aware and informed of what awaits Him in Jerusalem. See Him steadfast in heart, determined, setting the pace for His disciples, striding purposefully forward.

Where?

To Jerusalem.

Why?

To die.

He will not be deterred. He's full of resolve as He keeps this appointment made in eternity past. Relentlessly He proceeds to a place where He'll be betrayed and arrested, where He'll be accused and condemned, where He'll be mocked and spit upon and flogged and ultimately executed. And there's no hesitation, no reluctance in His steps. Though unimaginable suffering is before Him, He's walking ahead, *leading the way.*

THE RANSOM

This then is the background for Jesus' encounter with the proud words and actions of His arrogant and indignant disciples. And as He confronts their pride—and our own—Jesus for the first time defines the purpose of His approaching death and what it will accomplish: "The Son of Man came...to give his life as a ransom for many" (Mark 10:45).

Earlier in this chapter, Mark has provided additional information that deepens the meaning of this profound moment: Not long before this time, Jesus had encountered a rich young ruler who wanted to know how to earn eternal life. After hearing the Savior's answer, the disciples had been "exceedingly astonished" and had asked Him, "Then who can be saved?" Jesus had looked at them and replied, "With man it is impossible, but not with God. For all things are possible with God" (v. 27).

Having revealed the impossibility of salvation apart from God, now Jesus is revealing *how* God will save. The Savior describes His coming death as a "ransom." He's intentional and strategic in His use of that word.

Unfortunately, *ransom* has a fairly limited meaning to us. We don't encounter it much except while watching TV shows or movies with a kidnapping in the plot. But the meaning of this word was much more intense and immediate and familiar to the disciples that day. As Donald English reminds us, "*Ransom* was a familiar image in the Jewish, Roman, and Greek cultures. It was the price paid to liberate a slave, a prisoner of war, or a condemned person."[2] A ransom represented the payment of a price required for deliverance from various forms of bondage, captivity, or condemnation that were common in those days.

MISSING RESPECTABILITY

Moreover, *ransom* wasn't a term associated with respectability. The person being ransomed was either a slave, an imprisoned enemy, or a condemned criminal.

How does that apply to us? Only too well. As John Stott writes, the emphasis of the ransom image "is on our sorry state—indeed our captivity in sin—which made the act of divine rescue necessary."[3] That's the focus revealed here. So to hear the Savior speak the word *ransom* and understand it rightly is to be freshly reminded and affected by our own serious and sorry state, our miserable lostness and wretched bondage to sin. We *cannot* free ourselves from pride and selfish ambition; a divine rescue is absolutely necessary.

Jesus is seeking to impress this message on each one of us: "You're lost. Your situation couldn't be more hopeless. And on your own, you're incapable of altering or escaping it."

Why was the death of Jesus necessary? Because all of humanity is corrupt and condemned, and we all have an acute tendency to deny the reality of our lost state before God.

HERE WE ARE

To clarify the seriousness of our plight, we need look no further than here in Mark 10. Observe carefully and you'll find your own face among the various portraits Mark provides in this passage of Scripture.

Perhaps you recognize yourself in the rich young ruler who valued his possessions more highly than the Savior's words. Perhaps you see yourself in James and John and their selfish ambitions. Or, if you consider yourself superior to James and John and their attitude, then you'll fit among the other disciples in their indignation, which revealed not only their own desire for glory but also their self-righteousness—possibly a far more serious sin than James and John's.

But let me be clear. *All* of us appear somewhere in Mark's portrait gallery of sinners. And Jesus Himself drives home for us what that means—a humanly unalterable condition of captivity to sin.

Our situation couldn't be more serious. Prior to our conversion we were sin's prisoners, and even after our conversion we continue to fight the presence of sin, though we're freed from the power and penalty of sin. And if you aren't aware of this danger, you'll never sufficiently appreciate the significance of His death. It's this captivity to sin and continued tendency to sin that necessitates the Savior's death as a *ransom for many*. That's the price the ransom requires: the life of God's only Son.

It was humanly impossible for the disciples to free themselves from their selfish pursuit of self-exaltation, just as it's impossible for us to free ourselves from the very same sins. But God accomplishes that which is humanly impossible! He pays the price for our freedom, and that price is the sinless Son of God's substitutionary sacrifice on the cross.

THE GOOD NEWS

How will God save? He will save by executing His Son—for the sake of rich young rulers, for the sake of James and John, for the sake of ten indignant disciples, and for the sake of proud sinners like you and me. How will God free us from the prison of pride? How can we be liberated from the dominating power of the world's empty definitions of greatness?

For those who feel the effect of their serious condition, who realize their humanly unalterable condition, the good news is that there's One who appears on the scene and says this: "I've come. I'm leading the way. I'm moving relentlessly to the place where I'll be nailed to a cross and lifted up as the ultimate example of suffering, and there the concentrated fury of the Father's wrath for *your* sins will be visited upon *Me*. And I will groan, for I am sinless and I'm unfamiliar with *any* sin, with even a single sin. Yet on that cross I will experience the sins of many visited upon My body. And I will die."

This is the death that awaits Him. But joy will follow His suffering: the certain joy of knowing His death has ransomed the many!

That's the effect of the atoning death of the Son of God.

IF GOD WANTS US BACK...

Leon Morris describes our humanly unalterable condition in this way:

> God created man, created him to be His own.... God set him in Eden to live in fellowship with Him, but man sinned. Man became the slave of evil. He cannot break free. This is precisely the situation that the ancient world saw as calling for an act of redemption. We who belong to God have gotten into the power of a strong enemy from which we cannot break free. If I can say it reverently, God, if He wants us back, must pay the price.
>
> And the great teaching of the New Testament is that God has paid the price. He has redeemed us. Christ became our Redeemer.... To release the slaves of sin He paid the price. We were in captivity. We were in the strong grip of evil. We could not break free. But the price was paid and the result is that we go free.[4]

That's exactly right. *We do go free!* We're ransomed...liberated...forgiven of our sins. What a relief!

And then we're transformed throughout our lifetimes

into the image of His Son, serving others for the glory of God. That's the effect of this sacrifice: Many are ransomed, many are transformed. Including James and John. Because this account in Mark 10 is not the final chapter in their story.

JAMES AND JOHN TRANSFORMED

James and John were ransomed by the Savior's death and forgiven of their pride and all their sins. And they would be transformed as well, from self-confident men into humble servants who would live to serve others with the gospel for the glory of God.

And they would suffer.

After Christ's resurrection and ascension, James was the first of the apostles to be martyred, as we read early in the book of Acts: "About that time Herod the king laid violent hands on some who belonged to the church. He killed James the brother of John with the sword" (Acts 12:1–2).

Scripture tells us, "Precious in the sight of the LORD is the death of his saints" (Psalm 116:15). How profoundly precious in His eyes must have been the sight of this once self-confident and selfishly ambitious man kneeling down while the executioner's sword was raised above him! What had transformed James? What had happened between Mark 10 and Acts 12?

The Savior had died as a ransom.

John, his brother, would be transformed as well. John was apparently the last of all the apostles to die, but he suffered persecution and was banished to the island of Patmos. It's obvious from the letters John wrote that he understood his Savior's teaching on humble servanthood: "By this we know love, that [Christ] laid down his life for us, and we ought to lay down our lives for the brothers" (1 John 3:16). John got it right.

What transformed John? What had happened between Mark 10 and the writing of John's epistles?

The Savior had died as a ransom.

The James and John we see back in Mark 10 were emphatically *not* laying down their lives for others, but they would be wholly transformed. And the explanation for this transformation wasn't just our Lord's example but our Lord's *sacrifice*. His sacrifice was a ransom for sin, and its effect was a liberation for James and John from their selfishness and patterns of pride.

Here were two men transformed into humble servants of the gospel and servants of the church by the Savior's sacrifice. Two men who ended their lives truly great in the eyes of God.

Why? How?

"The Son of Man came not to be served but to serve, and to give his life as a ransom for many" (Matthew 20:28).

SEEING THE SOURCE

As you encounter those who humbly serve, know that they're truly great in the eyes of God. But understand also the source of their serving. Their humble service should remind you of *this* death, *this* ransom, *this* price paid to liberate the one whom you now see serving.

Consider your own life for just a moment. Where would *you* be today if He hadn't ransomed you, if He hadn't liberated you? I'll tell you where. You would be self-sufficient, seeking to cultivate self-confidence for the purpose of self-glorification.

But what has happened to you? If you've been genuinely converted, you've been forgiven and *transformed*. And though for now there remains in you a temptation and tendency to sin, a fundamental and radical change has occurred so that you have the desire to serve others and to see God glorified. We know the inner call to lay down our lives for one another *because He laid down His life for us.*

What a powerful death! The cross ransoms, the cross liberates, the cross transforms! So make it your aim and lifelong habit, when you see someone who's serving, to be reminded of the sacrifice of the Savior, for *apart from His sacrifice there is no serving.* True greatness is attained only by emulating the Savior's example—and made possible only by the Savior's sacrifice.

Notes

1. Donald English, *The Message of Mark: The Mystery of Faith* (Downers Grove, IL: InterVarsity Press, 1992), 182.
2. Ibid.
3. John Stott, *The Cross of Christ* (Downers Grove, IL: InterVarsity Press, 1986), 175.
4. Leon Morris, *The Atonement: Its Meaning and Significance* (Downers Grove, IL: InterVarsity Press, 1984), 120–21.

PART III

OUR GREAT PURSUIT

The Practice of True Humility

5

AS EACH DAY BEGINS

HERE'S A SCARY THOUGHT: It's possible to admire humility while remaining proud ourselves. I'm very aware that it's possible for me even now to be teaching on humility while neglecting pride in my own heart. And at this moment you may be deceiving yourself into thinking that you are making progress against pride simply because you are reading a book about humility. (Though I hope that's not true!)

OUR NEED FOR PURPOSEFUL APPLICATION

Merely being inspired by the promise of humility or the meaning of true greatness is not sufficient; nor is it enough to also be educated about the perils of pride. If there's ever to be meaningful transformation in our lives, if we are to make progress in restraining pride and manifesting humility, *there must be the purposeful application of truth*—an effort and pursuit on our part that God will use for sanctifying transformation in our lives.

Remember again John Stott's wise instruction: In every step of our Christian growth and maturity, and throughout every aspect of our Christian obedience and service, our greatest foe is pride and our greatest ally is humility.

I'm convinced of this from Scripture, and out of that certainty and conviction I must consider how I can daily, diligently, and deliberately weaken my greatest enemy and strengthen my greatest friend—all motivated by grace in the shadow of the cross.

A PRACTICAL STRATEGY

In the rest of this book, I want to explore with you an extended list of practical ways I have found to weaken pride and cultivate humility—to help me tremble at His Word and help me stay focused on pursuing true greatness.

The items on this list aren't something I've simply jotted down in the last month or so, but something I began developing privately a few decades ago. They've grown out of my life as pursuits that have gradually and progressively pressed upon my heart and mind over the last thirty years of seeking to grow in grace. And they've proven consistently helpful.

For your own purposes, think of the items on my list simply as recommendations, not requirements—as suggestions for your consideration. Don't think I'm trying to promote some strict emulation of my practices. These are for your deliberation and reflection; after weighing their value, you need to custom-design your own list.

But let me impress this on you: *You should have a list.* You should be purposeful about this. Each day you should be planning the defeat of your greatest enemy and cultivating your greatest friend.

Some of these items on my list are daily practices, relatively brief actions and responses that anyone can do regularly and repeatedly. I think of them as ways to discipline my day or my daily routine with the goal of trembling at God's Word, weakening pride, and developing humility. Other items on the list are endeavors that require more time; they're longer-term pursuits that could stretch over the next year or two or more, but with the same goal of attacking pride and fortifying humility.

REFLECT ON THE WONDER OF THE CROSS

For me, the most consistently helpful item on the list is this: *Reflect on the wonder of the cross of Christ.* I believe this will be the most important habit and practice for you as well. To truly be serious and deliberate in mortifying pride and cultivating greatness, you must each day survey the wondrous cross on which the Prince of Glory died.

"Fill your affections with the cross of Christ," wrote John Owen, "that there may be no room for sin."[1] And that includes no room for pride.

Martyn Lloyd-Jones wrote the following about the surest way to pursue humility:

> There is only one thing I know of that crushes me to the ground and humiliates me to the dust, and that is to look at the Son of God, and especially contemplate the cross.
>
> > When I survey the wondrous cross
> > On which the Prince of Glory died,
> > My richest gain I count but loss
> > And pour contempt on all my pride
>
> Nothing else can do it. When I see that I am a sinner…that nothing but the Son of God on the cross can save me, I'm humbled to the dust…. Nothing but the cross can give us this spirit of humility.[2]

John Stott helps us understand why the cross has this powerful effect:

> Every time we look at the cross Christ seems to be saying to us, "I am here because of you. It is your sin I am bearing, your curse I am suffering, your debt I am paying, your death I am dying." Nothing in history or in the universe cuts us down to size like the cross. All of us have inflated views of ourselves, especially in self-righteousness, until we have visited a place called Calvary. It is there, at the foot of the cross, that we shrink to our true size.[3]

I once had the privilege of spending an hour with Don Carson, Bible scholar and professor at Trinity Evangelical Seminary. In the course of our conversation, he told me of an interview he had with the late Carl Henry, perhaps the foremost evangelical theologian of the latter half of the twentieth century. Dr. Henry was characterized by not only brilliance but also humility—a rare combination. So Dr. Carson asked him how he had remained humble for so many decades.

Listening to Dr. Carson, I sat poised with pen and paper, ready to record Carl Henry's answer. This was it:

"How can anyone be arrogant when he stands beside the cross?"

So many times since that conversation, I've thought, *Father, I want to stand as close to the cross as I possibly can, because it's harder for me to be arrogant when I'm there.*

The cross never flatters us. Stott also wrote, "Far from offering us flattery, the cross undermines our self-righteousness, and we can stand before it only with a bowed head and a broken spirit."[4]

To further help you stand closer to the cross on a daily basis, I recommend that you read *The Cross of Christ* by John Stott or *The Gospel for Real Life* by Jerry Bridges. Books such as these help us, as Charles Spurgeon once put it, to "abide close to the cross, and search the mystery of His wounds"[5] as we meditate on the Savior's glorious atonement and cultivate humility in the process.

BEGIN YOUR DAY ACKNOWLEDGING YOUR NEED FOR GOD

For the rest of this chapter, I want to focus on humility-inducing practices to build into your life at the beginning of each day. How we begin our morning so often sets the tone for the day. I'm convinced that the most decisive time of our day is very often our first waking moments, because they color everything to come.

The first daily item from my list is this: *Begin your day by acknowledging your dependence upon God and your need for God*. Purpose by grace that your first thought of the day will be an expression of your dependence on God, your need for God, and your confidence in God.

Sin—including especially the sin of pride—is active, not passive. Sin doesn't wake up tired, because it hasn't been sleeping. When you wake up in the morning, sin is right there, fully awake, ready to attack. So rather than be attacked by sin in the morning, I've chosen to go on the offensive. I've chosen to announce to sin, "I'm at war with you. I know you're there, and I'm after you." From the moment I awake, I've learned to make statements *to* God about my dependence *upon* God, and in this way I'm humbling myself *before* God.

This is simply a strategy for taking control of the thoughts we allow in our mind. In his excellent book *Spiritual Depression,* Martyn Lloyd-Jones asked, "Have you realized that most of your unhappiness in life is due to the fact that you are listening to yourself instead of talking to yourself?"[6] That's profound, and it's true.

Take a moment to review and examine your pattern of thinking from yesterday. Did you spend more time speaking truth to yourself, or was most of your time spent listening to yourself? Most of us spend more time listening to lies than we do speaking truth to ourselves. And the listening process usually starts as soon as we get up. The alarm has rudely interrupted the gift of sleep, and the listening begins. As we stumble through our morning routine, we're not directing the thoughts in our mind—we're simply at their mercy. We entertain complaints about what happened yesterday or worries about what's coming today. We look in the bathroom mirror and assess the damage, then brood over how we feel. We're not in charge of our thinking. We're just there.

But instead, you can declare war on pride by speaking the truth to yourself and set the right tone for your day by mentally affirming your dependence upon God and your need for Him.

BEGIN YOUR DAY EXPRESSING GRATITUDE TO GOD

The second daily item is this: *Begin your day expressing gratefulness to God.*

"Thankfulness," Michael Ramsey reminds us, "is a soil in which pride does not easily grow."[7] That's exactly right and we want to cultivate that soil. So from the outset of the day, I want to greet my Savior with gratitude, not grumbling.

It was said of Matthew Henry that "he was an alert and thankful observer of answered prayer"; his gratitude for

God's mercies was constantly "sweetening his spirit, and he would often invite others to join him in giving thanks."[8] If you crossed Matthew Henry's path, you would quickly realize that here was someone taking thankful notice of all God was doing for him, and doing so in an attractively joyful way that was infectious.

How I want that to also be a description of me! Is this your desire as well?

What would happen if I crossed your path tomorrow morning? Would I encounter someone who was an alert and thankful observer of answered prayer, someone who in a pronounced way was grateful for God's many mercies?

We also want to continue throughout the day expressing gratefulness for the innumerable manifestations of God's grace. It's as if God is placing sticky-notes in our lives as daily reminders of His presence and provision. They're everywhere. How alert and perceptive of them are you? Are you a thankful observer of the countless indications of His provision, His presence, His kindness, and His grace?

An ungrateful person is a proud person. If I'm ungrateful, I'm arrogant. And if I'm arrogant, I need to remember God doesn't sympathize with me in that arrogance; He is opposed to the proud.

Let each of us recognize every day that whatever grace we receive from God is so much more than we're worthy of, and indescribably better than the hell we all deserve.

PRACTICE SPIRITUAL DISCIPLINES

The next habit: *Practice the spiritual disciplines*—prayer, study of God's Word, worship. Do this consistently each day, preferably at the day's outset, if possible. If we're properly motivated, this will be a daily demonstration and declaration of our dependence on God and our need for Him.

I've found that it's possible for me to charge into my day motivated by self-sufficiency. But I've also learned that the very act of opening my Bible to read and turning my heart and mind to prayer makes a statement that I need God. I find great benefit from this understanding, because like you, I have wildly fluctuating emotional experiences from day to day in my devotions. One morning I'm profoundly aware that God is near to me, while the next day I can sense only His absence. In a matter of hours I go from what seems to be an effortless experience of pure joy to asking, "Where are You? Where did You go?"

The fact is, of course, He didn't go anywhere. Yesterday He allowed me to sense His presence; today He seems to be sending the message, "I want you to grow more in your trust in Me; therefore, I'm withdrawing that sense of My nearness."

I've learned that regardless of how I feel when I'm finished reading my Bible in the morning, I can know that I've made the statement, "I need You, I'm dependent upon

You." By quietly pausing to study and read and pray before launching my workday, I can be confident that I've taken a step to weaken pride and strengthen humility.

The finest book I've read on this topic is *Spiritual Disciplines for the Christian Life* by Donald S. Whitney, and I recommend it to you.

Seize Your Commute

Something else to consider doing each morning: *Seize your commute time to memorize and meditate on Scripture*.

On a daily basis, commute time probably represents the biggest portion of wasted time in our culture. Tomorrow morning, the sun will rise in the DC area where I live, and tomorrow morning the traffic on the Beltway will be backed up. And yet thousands of people will sit in their cars reacting as if something shocking and unexpected were happening, even though it's been going on for decades. And what will they sit there doing? Complaining.

If you have a long commute, how do you spend the time?

According to government figures from census information, the average American worker commutes about twenty-five minutes to and from work. That amounts to fifty minutes in the car each weekday. If you used that time to listen to an audio recording of Scripture, you'd get through the entire Bible in only three months!

Even if you don't have a long commute, there are countless other segments of time throughout the day—I think of them as *mundane moments*—that can be seized as opportunities to experience God's transforming grace by memorizing and meditating on Scripture.

In the nineteenth century, the evangelical statesman William Wilberforce was largely responsible for the end of England's participation in the slave trade. John Piper has written and spoken much about this hero of the faith, and he tells how Wilberforce used his one-mile walk to and from Parliament, where he served in the House of Commons, to memorize and meditate on Psalm 119. Wilberforce could recite the entire psalm in the course of the one-mile walk. He seized that time to speak truth to himself, not listen to himself.

For so many of us, our commute is wasted every day. You can either get into mental ruts during this time, or seize your commute time as a means of grace to allow Scripture to transform your thinking.

CASTING YOUR CARES UPON HIM

The final item for each morning (and something to come back to throughout your day): *Cast your cares upon Him.* The apostle Peter clearly and practically describes for us how we can humble ourselves daily in 1 Peter 5:6–7. First he writes, "Humble yourselves, therefore, under the mighty hand of God." Then he shows us *how:* "casting all your anxieties on him, because he cares for you."

When we humble ourselves each morning by casting all our cares on the Lord, we will start the day free of care. The humble are genuinely care free.

I've discovered how true that is about myself and my soul. Where there's worry, where there's anxiousness, *pride* is at the root of it. When I am experiencing anxiety, the root issue is that I'm trying to be self-sufficient. I'm acting independent of God.

What's the solution?

"Humble yourself," God says.

How?

"Acknowledge your need for Me! Cast your cares upon Me, and I will transform you, C. J. For though I'm opposed to your pride, I'll give grace to you when you humble yourself, and I'll make you care free—not responsibility free, but care free. You'll be free from care. You'll instead be characterized by joy and peace."

STAYING CHARGED UP

We have to focus on this daily, because we're not like cordless drills, getting charged up in the morning with enough power to last us the rest of the day. We have to keep a prayerful attitude through the day, constantly bringing to Him whatever care we encounter, whatever anxiety-producing responsibility comes our way.

Maybe you've wondered why your devotions in the morning sometimes seem to be effective for only an hour or so. I've learned not to expect that what I've experienced in Bible study in the morning will be sustaining me at two-thirty in the afternoon. No, by two-thirty in the afternoon, someone will have brought me a care (or more likely, a number of people will have done so). And this requires deliberately approaching the Lord to cast those cares upon Him.

I have to remember that whenever I feel buried under care, the real issue is pride and my self-sufficiency. I must deliberately and specifically cast my cares upon Him and thereby humble myself.

Don't be mistaken. God hasn't gone anywhere. He's just as sovereign, just as good, just as faithful when I'm buried under care as He was in those early hours of communion. The issue isn't God. It's my pride that resists trusting in Him through dependence upon Him.

In fact, I should also recognize that all the cares coming my way are actually provided by God specifically for the purpose of cultivating humility in my life. I shouldn't act surprised when they come, because there's a reason.

God wants me to learn to depend on Him, to need Him, and in the end, to give glory to Him with an ever-deepening appreciation for the mighty hand of God.

So I advocate using your morning moments wisely, letting the light of God's grace shine in to brighten your entire day. I'm convinced that your purposeful application of these daily morning habits—acknowledging your need for God; expressing your gratitude to God; practicing spiritual disciplines; seizing your commute time for spiritual benefit; casting your cares upon Him; and above all, reflecting on the wonder of the cross of Christ—are *the* most effective things you can do to more deeply experience the promise and the pleasures of humility.

Notes
1. John Owen, from his treatise on "Indwelling Sin," http://www.godrules.net/library/owen/131-295owen_f4.htm (accessed August 3, 2005).
2. Martyn Lloyd-Jones, as quoted in Charles Swindoll, *So You Want to Be Like Christ? Eight Essentials to Get You There* (Nashville, TN: W Publishing Group, 2005), 139.
3. John Stott, *The Message of Galatians* (Downers Grove, IL; InterVarsity Press, 1968), 179.
4. John Stott, *The Cross of Christ* (Downers Grove, IL: InterVarsity Press, 1986), 12.
5. Charles H. Spurgeon, *Morning and Evening* (New Kensington, PA: Whitaker House, 2001), 7.

6. Martyn Lloyd-Jones, *Spiritual Depression* (Grand Rapids, MI: Eerdmans, 1965), 20.

7. Michael Ramsey, *The Christian Priest Today* (London: SPCK, 1972) 79–81; as quoted in John Stott, "Pride, Humility & God," in *Alive to God*, eds. J. I. Packer and Loren Wilinson (Downers Grover, IL: InterVarsity, 1992), 112.

8. Ligon Duncan, as quoted in Matthew Henry, *Method for Prayer* (Ross-shire: Christian Focus, 1994), introduction.

6

As Each Day Ends

There's another set of helpful practices on my list that focus especially on the end of my day. This is a reminder we especially need, because few of us have thought biblically and strategically about how to glorify God at the end the day—even though the way we end today can clearly affect the way we encounter tomorrow. We're familiar with the importance of practicing spiritual disciplines in the morning, but most of us aren't aware of any specific biblical instruction about how to conclude each day.

The end of each day offers us a unique opportunity to cultivate humility and weaken pride, as well as to sense God's pleasure. How? By reviewing our day and carefully assigning all glory to God for the grace we've experienced that day.

You see, throughout each day we're experiencing saving grace, sanctifying grace, sustaining grace, serving grace—grace that should amaze us. But what's often happening in our minds as we plunge into our pillows? We're trying not to think about the unpleasant tasks that await us tomorrow! Or if we're reflecting at all on the blessings we've experienced that day, we're failing to express gratefulness to God and assign all glory to the only One truly worthy of it.

"When we have done anything praiseworthy," wrote the Puritan giant Thomas Watson, "we must hide ourselves under the veil of humility, and transfer the glory of all we have done to God."[1]

Of course, you don't have to wait until day's end to do this. Do it *all* day, throughout the day, every day. But let not a single day end without the specific and intentional "transfer" of all glory, for all grace, to God alone! This is the humble way to end each and every day.

AVOIDING COSMIC PLAGIARISM

In recent years a couple of popular historians, whose writings I've enjoyed, were accused of plagiarism in their works. When I saw the reports of it, my initial reaction was to think, *How could they? Why would they?* But as I reflected on this, I was reminded that every time I claim to be the "author" in my life and ministry of that which is actually God's gift, I'm committing cosmic plagiarism. And that's far more serious than any alleged misconduct by those two historians.

So what must I do?

By grace I must intentionally transfer the glory to God.

The encouragement I receive from those I have the privilege of ministering to is overwhelming to me. I believe their expressions of encouragement are pleasing to God. As I thank them for their kind words I quietly transfer the glory to God. I know that in my ministry I can't change anybody's life. I have no power for that. When others describe changes that have taken place through my preaching or my leadership, I'm deeply aware that I simply don't have that kind of ability or power.

Yes, leaders are vital to the church, and it's appropriate to thank those leaders who have been used by God as a means of His grace. But we're to ascribe glory to no man. Glory is ascribed exclusively and entirely to God. Only He can regenerate a heart. Only He can change a life. Therefore, only God should receive glory.

Whatever successes you experience in your life and ministry and vocation, learn to immediately transfer the glory to Him. If your business is successful, are you trans-ferring the glory for that success to Him? If people compliment you for your effective parenting, do you transfer the glory to Him? Recognize that though you're a means of grace to your children, you can't in and of yourself transform your children—only God can. And as He does, only He gets the glory.

ACCEPT THE GIFT OF SLEEP

Another significant end-of-the-day entry to put into practice before you doze off: *Receive the gift of sleep from God and acknowledge His purpose for sleep.*

My wife, Carolyn, and I have been married for thirty grace-filled, passionately romantic years, and for the first twenty-seven of those years we slept on the original bed frame and box springs that we started with. At night we just kind of tumbled in together and met in the middle; it was like a water bed without any water.

Before we finally got rid of it, there were moments when I stopped and stared at that bed. I knew that on average we all spend nearly a third of our lives asleep, and so I was struck by the fact that about nine years of my life had been spent in that bed. Nine years!

I was struck also by the fact that Scripture talks about those nine years. Do you realize how often sleep is referred to in Scripture? We shouldn't be surprised at this, because God is sovereign over all of life, as David declared: "The earth is the LORD's and the fullness thereof" (Psalm 24:1).

God created and provided sleep. So for the remaining years that I'll spend in bed, I am determined to keep a biblical perspective of sleep; therefore, I want to glorify God each night as I close my eyes.

Too many Christians fall asleep night after night without being informed and inspired by what Scripture teaches on it. Many of us have never considered our sleep from God's perspective, though we profess to love and serve Him; our practice and perspective regarding sleep are no different from that of non-Christians. This needs to change.

A Christian, informed and inspired by Scripture, views the cessation of work each day, the limitation God places upon work each day, and the laying down to sleep each night, as altogether *a gift from God*. A gift so graciously provided in His lavish generosity. And those who neglect this gift will inevitably suffer consequences.

A Daily Reminder from God

The benefits of sleep are obvious. As we sleep, strength is restored, the mind is cleared, and we're prepared to serve God another day—to rise and experience His mercies that are new every morning. What a wonderful gift to be given on a daily basis!

The fact is, God could have created us without a need

for sleep. But He chose to build this need within us, and there's a spiritual purpose for it. Each night, as I confront my need again for sleep, I'm reminded that I'm a dependent creature. I am not self-sufficient. I am not the Creator. There is only One who "will neither slumber nor sleep" (Psalm 121:4), and I am not that One.

Sleep is a gift, but it's a humbling one. It's a matter of only hours, at most, before you're ready to again receive God's gift of sleep. When that time comes, let me encourage you to pray something like this: "Lord, thank You for this gift. The fact that I'm so tired is a reminder that I am the creature and only You are the Creator. Only You neither slumber nor sleep, while for me, sleep is something I cannot go without. Thank You for this gracious, humbling, refreshing gift."

A PICTURE AND A PARABLE

If possible, make your final thought each night an expression of gratefulness for the Savior's sacrifice on the cross as your substitute for your many sins. This is what I try to do each night, and I commend this practice to you.

My good friend Mark Dever once reminded me that sleep is a picture and a parable of what it means to be a Christian. Your sleep tonight will be a small but real act of faith. You'll lay your full weight on a bed, trusting this structure to support you. You can fully relax, because no effort at supporting yourself is required; something else is holding you up. And in the same way, throughout the night as you sleep, *Someone else is sustaining you.* This is a picture of what it's like to belong to Christ.

I've been a Christian for more than thirty years, and I've learned that my going to sleep each night is really a picture and a parable of my life-experience since that late-summer day in 1972 when God granted me the miracle of regeneration through the proclamation of His gospel. Before that moment I was an object of His wrath; but in the mystery of His mercy, I was immediately transformed into an object of His mercy as I trusted Jesus Christ with every aspect of my life, beginning with forgiveness for my sins, as well as all my hopes for the future.

Sleep is a gift that God makes available to all humanity. It's another of the innumerable illustrations of His extravagant generosity not only toward His people but even toward those who are hostile and opposed to Him. And we, as His own people, should not only thank Him but also respond fully and appropriately and humbly in receiving this gift.

So don't just fall asleep tonight or any night. Seize this opportunity to mortify pride and cultivate humility by setting apart sleep as a holy gift from God, as a reminder of your full dependence on Him and as an occasion to examine your heart before Him. Let the Spirit give you a new perception and appreciation of sleep, so that this seemingly ordinary act might be transformed into an opportunity to cultivate humility and weaken pride.

Notes

1. Thomas Watson, *Body of Divinity* (Edinburgh: Banner of Truth, 1998), n.p.

7

For Special Focus

To help us cultivate humility and weaken pride, these next few recommended practices will move us beyond our daily routines. The practices in this chapter have to do with times of special focus—things that you give extended concentration to. So as you read on, I recommend that you be fully alert and, if necessary, fully caffeinated. Challenging content lies ahead! But I'm confident these suggestions will prove as richly rewarding for you as they have been for me.

Study the Attributes of God

Number one on this section of my list: *Study the attributes of God.*

Study all of His attributes, but I recommend you study in particular what the theologians have identified as the *incommunicable* attributes of God. These are the attributes of God for which no human reflection or human illustration can be found. They're attributes that God doesn't share with us.

When we say, for example, that God is infinite, we're speaking of an incommunicable attribute—God doesn't share this quality with us. God alone is infinite, free of all limitations of space and distance. As the *New Bible Dictionary* expresses it, "When we say that God is infinite in spirit, we pass completely out of the reach of our experience."[1] Yes, we do.

God is omnipresent—everywhere equally present. Just think about that for a moment. There's no place where He isn't fully present. I, on the other hand, can only be in one place at any given time, and even then I'm not always fully there!

God is also absolutely self-existent and self-sufficient. Of this attribute, R. C. Sproul writes:

> The grand difference between a human being and a supreme being is precisely this: Apart from God, I cannot exist. Apart from me, God does exist. God does not need me in order for Him to be; I do need God in order for me to be. This is the difference between what we call self-existent being

and dependent being. We are dependent. We are fragile. We cannot live without air, without water, without food. No human being has the power of being within himself. Life is lived between two hospitals. We need a support system from birth to death to sustain life. We are like flowers that bloom and then wither and then fade. This is how we differ from God. God does not wither, God does not fade, God is not fragile.[2]

Matthew Henry expressed it this way: "The greatest and best man in the world must say, By the grace of God *I am what I am*, but God says absolutely...*I am that I am*."[3]

As we investigate such attributes, we become increasingly aware of the indescribably vast distance between ourselves and God. Ironically, this distance from God will be even more real to us when we get "closer" to God in heaven, as Jonathan Edwards reminds us: "The saints in glory are so much employed in praise, because they are perfect in *humility*, and have so great a sense of the infinite distance between them and God."[4]

Even now, the more you're aware of this distance and this difference between you and God, the more you will experience and express humility, and you'll say with David, "Such knowledge is too wonderful for me; it is high; I cannot attain it" (Psalm 139:6).

Therefore, I urge you in the coming months to devote yourself to the study of the incommunicable attributes of God. For help here, it doesn't get any better than Wayne Grudem's *Systematic Theology*. Or find the abridged version, entitled *Bible Doctrine*. In both editions you'll find a chapter on God's incommunicable attributes, with the subtitle "How Is God Different from Us?" Read this chapter and I believe it will have a profound effect on your heart.

Study the Doctrines of Grace

Number two on my list of longer-term pursuits: *Study the doctrines of grace*. Study the doctrines of election, calling, justification, perseverance—and the effect will be humility. Why? Because the doctrines of grace leave no room for self-congratulation, no room for self-glorification.

For example, Mark Webb notes how the doctrine of election curbs our pride:

God intentionally designed salvation so that no man can boast of it. He didn't merely arrange it so that boasting would be discouraged, or kept to a minimum—He planned it so that boasting would be absolutely excluded! Election does precisely that.[5]

That's exactly right.

And the same is true for all the doctrines that concern our salvation. Consider the doctrine of our "calling." Fundamentally, we're Christians because God called us—sovereignly, graciously, mercifully, effectively—not because we called out to Him. Our calling upon Him was preceded and made possible by His calling us! That's humbling.

Or take the doctrine of our "justification." We're justified before God—declared righteous in His sight—not on the basis of our moral performance but on the basis of the perfect performance of His Son. This is the very design of the gospel, "so that no human being might boast in the presence of God" (1 Corinthians 1:29). That's humbling, too.

Then there's the doctrine of our "perseverance." We'll persevere in our faith until the end of our lives not from human strength, but because Jesus is preserving us, holding us tightly in His strong hands. That, too, is humbling.

Our salvation, from first to last, is truly all of grace—and the effect of this grace understood is humility.

To understand these doctrines more, let me recommend that you read *Saved by Grace* by Anthony Hoekema.

STUDY THE DOCTRINE OF SIN

And finally, among these longer-term pursuits: *Study the doctrine of sin.*

I heard about a sign on a department store dressing room mirror that read, "Objects in mirror may appear bigger than they actually are." That will not be your experience in studying the doctrine of sin; you will never appear bigger than you actually are.

John Owen writes, "There are two things that are suited to humble the souls of men.... A due consideration of God, and then of ourselves. Of God, in his greatness, glory, holiness, power, majesty and authority; of ourselves, in our mean, abject and sinful condition."[6] Those would be included in God's incommunicable attributes, as we discussed earlier—so study those first.

There's no one, by the way, who can assist you more effectively in the study of your "mean, abject, and sinful condition" than John Owen himself. If you really want to do a number on pride, read his *Sin and Temptation* either in the original or the abridged version. Let me recommend as well that you read *The Enemy Within: Straight Talk About the Power and Defeat of Sin* by Kris Lundgaard, which is a wonderful introduction to the writings of Owen and the doctrine of sin.

We need to study sin and become more aware of its ways, because so often we're simply imperceptive of sin's presence. Why is that? Hebrews 3:13 tells us to guard against being "hardened by the deceitfulness of sin." It's the very nature of sin to be deceitful. Sin is subtle and difficult to discern, especially the sin of pride. And it has a gradual hardening effect on the soul.

Sin always has a destructive effect, but often that effect isn't immediately obvious. Over a period of time, however, where sin is indulged, there'll be a hardening effect on the soul of a genuinely converted Christian.

To differing degrees we're all familiar with this hardening effect. Perhaps you gradually find yourself less affected by corporate worship in your local church. Or you've recently noticed that your appetite for Holy Scripture has diminished. You may be less sensitive to sin, or your confession of sin is less frequent and lacks sorrow.

The ultimate effect from such hardening by sin is that grace, for the Christian, is no longer amazing. That's why we need to stay close to the doctrine of sin—because it helps us see the presence of pride and protects us from those hardening effects. The doctrine of sin was specifically designed for this, and it's sufficiently potent to put pride to death in our lives by the power of the Holy Spirit.

Regarding all these topics and doctrines mentioned in this chapter, remember that study alone isn't sufficient. Along with increased knowledge there must also be grace-motivated *application* of truth and grace-empowered obedience to truth. Only then will we experience Christ's liberating power from the sin of pride.

TWO MORE

Just in case this list is becoming a heavy load and you think I'm all study and no fun, let me add two unique suggestions for your extended focus and concentration. When you aren't exploring the attributes of God, the doctrines of grace, and the doctrine of sin, try these surefire methods for cultivating humility and weakening pride.

First, *play golf as much as possible.* Yep, golf. In my athletic experience, I don't think there's a more difficult or more humbling sport. Rather, make that *humiliating*—because if you play at all, you know all about those shots that result in laughter from your partners and humiliation for you. No one escapes them—not even Tiger Woods, and certainly not me.

Here's one more: *Laugh often, and laugh often at yourself.* After reading *Surprised by Laughter: The Comic World of C. S. Lewis* by Terry Lindvall, I've become aware of how much Lewis appreciated laughter. Inspired by his example, Lindvall writes this:

> Laughter is a divine gift to the human who is humble. A proud man cannot laugh because he

must watch his dignity; he cannot give himself over to the rocking and rolling of his belly. But a poor and happy man laughs heartily because he gives no serious attention to his ego.[7]

How about you? Are you making the most of this divine gift? I'm very grateful that God gave me a father with an unusual gift of humor, who taught me to laugh at myself (there's certainly no lack of material). Time and again laughter has provided much-needed help in my ongoing battle against pride.

There you have it: A few more practices you can pursue—some serious, some on the lighter side—to help you experience the joy of a humble life. So for the rest of your life, take time to study the attributes of God, the doctrines of grace, and the doctrine of sin, and play as much golf as you can.

And laugh, really laugh. Because funny stuff is happening all around you. (Sometimes *because* of you.)

Notes

1. Howard Marshall, ed., et al., *New Bible Dictionary*, 3rd ed., (Downers Grove, IL: InterVarsity Press).

2. R. C. Sproul, *One Holy Passion: The Consuming Thirst to Know God* (Nashville, TN: Thomas Nelson, 1989), 18.

3. *Matthew Henry's Concise Commentary on the Whole Bible* (Nashville, TN: Nelson Reference, 2000), commentary on Exodus 3.

4. Jonathan Edwards, "Praise, One of the Chief Employments of Heaven," in *The Works of Jonathan Edwards*, ed. Hickman (Edinburgh: Banner of Truth, 1974), 2:917.

5. Mark Webb, "What Difference Does It Make? A Discussion of the Evangelical Unity of the Doctrines of Grace." www.shilohonline.org/articles/webb/wddim.htm (accessed August 3, 2005).

6. John Owen, as quoted in J. I. Packer, *A Quest for Godliness: The Puritan Vision of the Christian Life* (Wheaton, IL: Crossway, 1990), 193.

7. Terry Lindvall, *Surprised by Laughter: The Comic World of C. S. Lewis* (Nashville, TN: Thomas Nelson, 1996), 130–31.

8

IDENTIFYING EVIDENCES OF GRACE

A CLASSIC *PEANUTS* CARTOON opens with Linus curled up in a chair, quietly reading a book, while Lucy stands behind him with a funny look on her face.

"It's very strange," Lucy tells him. "It happens just by looking at you."

"What happens?" Linus asks.

Lucy calmly answers, "I can feel a criticism coming on."

How often do you feel the same way when you look closely at those around you? The truth is, that's the tendency we all have apart from grace.

In Jane Austen's *Pride and Prejudice,* one of the central characters, Mr. Darcy, is described as a man "who never looks at any woman but to see a blemish."

How often do you function like Lucy or Mr. Darcy? Are you frequently critical of others? Do you look at those around you only to find one blemish after another? This proud tendency is a deeply rooted habit for many of us who have sown seeds of self-exaltation over the years.

This is why the next item on my list is such an important practice for cultivating humility: *Identify evidences of grace in others*. This means actively looking for ways that God is at work in the lives of other people.

THE EXAMPLE OF PAUL

The practice of identifying evidences of grace in others is drawn particularly from the opening nine verses of Paul's first letter to the Corinthians. I don't think a day goes by that I'm not influenced by this passage.

What we see here of Paul's godly attitude toward the Corinthian church and his sincere affection for the believers is a profound demonstration of the grace of God—and I use that word *profound* intentionally and emphatically. I find Paul's attitude here to be extraordinary.

It's likely that no church he served was ever in more desperate need of adjustment than this one at Corinth. This church was a piece of work. Consider the list of problems Paul had to address in his letter.

He speaks to a serious doctrinal error in which the Corinthians had drifted from the centrality of the cross and become seduced by human wisdom.

He addresses divisions within the church that had resulted in four emerging factions, all needing correction.

He addresses a form of immorality in their midst that would appall the average pagan but which incites only tolerance by the Corinthian church, a tolerance they're particularly proud of.

The Corinthians were a lawsuit-happy bunch as well, as Paul's admonishment tells us.

He also provides this stinging assessment of their corporate gatherings: "When you come together it is not for the better but for the worse" (1 Corinthians 11:17). When the Corinthians gathered for the Lord's Supper, some of them were drunk.

Meanwhile, the church at Corinth had also greatly misunderstood and misused the gifts of the Spirit, which Paul must address at length.

And to top it all off, there was broad opposition in this church to Paul himself and to his apostolic authority. It's difficult enough to guide a church as immature as this one; how much more challenging it must be when the church you're guiding is actively resisting your authority!

And yet in the opening lines of his letter, Paul communicates a passionate affection for this church that I find remarkable. He tells them, "I give thanks to my God *always* for you." Why? "Because of the grace of God that was given you in Christ Jesus" (1:4). Paul recognizes evidences of grace among the Corinthians, and he therefore continually thanks God for them.

THE BLINDNESS OF PRIDE

Personally, I wouldn't have wanted to be involved with this church. And had I been responsible for their spiritual growth and obligated to write them a letter, I doubt I would have started by saying, "I always thank God for you."

Why? Because I'm proud. And only those who are humble can consistently identify evidences of grace in others who need adjustment. It's something the proud and the self-righteous are incapable of.

But Paul, in his humility, saw the Corinthians from a divine perspective, and he allowed this perspective to determine his attitude toward them. And let me say by the authority of God's Word that you and I must hold this same perspective toward the believers around us. After all, if Paul can find evidences of overflowing grace even in the Corinthian church, what possible excuse could you and I have for our not finding evidences of grace in our fellow believers?

IDENTIFYING EVIDENCES OF GRACE

Where do we find and identify these evidences of grace? And how will we know them when we see them?

Here's where I encourage you to start: Be intimately familiar with the list of the fruit of the Spirit—"joy, peace, patience, kindness, goodness, faithfulness, gentleness, self-control" (Galatians 5:22–23). Make a practice of observing how the Spirit manifests these traits in the lives you see around you.

Likewise, familiarize yourself with the lists of the Spirit's gifts (see Romans 12:6–8; 1 Corinthians 12:8–10 and 12:28; Ephesians 4:11; 1 Peter 4:11) and observe the Spirit equipping believers to teach, to lead, and to serve. And remember that these lists aren't exhaustive but just a sampling of the gifting the Spirit provides.

When you become familiar with the fruit of the Spirit and the gifts of the Spirit and learn to recognize their manifestation, suddenly you will be aware that God is at work *everywhere!* Look anywhere and you'll see evidences of God's activity, evidences of grace. What a joy and privilege it is to discern this activity in the lives of those we love and care for—and to draw their attention to how God is at work in their lives.

SHAPING THIS DIVINE PERSPECTIVE

What went into shaping Paul's divine perspective, so that his eyes were wide open to see and appreciate the evidences of grace in the lives of the Corinthians?

Notice first that Paul uses the word "called" three times in the opening verses of 1 Corinthians. He's reminding us of God's initiative—we are all *called*. We're called to holiness and called into fellowship with Christ.

Sinclair Ferguson notes that *called* is one of Scripture's most frequent one-word descriptions for the Christian. In using it, Paul is especially acknowledging and affirming God's sovereign grace and reminding us of His prior activity: We were acted upon *by* God before we ever responded *to* Him.

Paul never minimizes or dismisses human responsibility. But the accent and emphasis both in his writings and throughout Scripture is upon the sovereignty of God, and out of it comes His call—His divine summons to which we respond. The fundamental explanation of our conversion was not that we were wiser or morally superior to others in choosing God, but that God chose to have mercy on us and intervened in our lives, revealing our need for His provision of the gospel. Our salvation is owed completely to the sovereign grace of God.

I can fully and personally agree with these words of Charles Spurgeon:

I believe in the doctrine of election, because I am quite certain that, if God had not chosen me, I should never have chosen Him; and I am sure He chose me before I was born, or else He never would have chosen me afterwards; and He must have elected me for reasons unknown to me, for I never could find any reason in myself why He should have looked upon me with special love.[1]

For Mr. Spurgeon, for me and you, to look back upon our conversion and explain fully and honestly how it came about, this fact must emerge: We were called. God's prior activity has brought us to where we are today.

The same is true of every believer we encounter. We must remind ourselves, *This individual has been previously acted upon by God.* That's the divine perspective we must begin with, or else we will be tempted to look for others' deficiencies rather than for the evidences of grace in their lives.

Paul knew the Corinthians had been called. He knew this church was the creation of God. And Paul was more aware of this prior activity of God than he was of their present failings. This fact sustained Paul by imparting faith for change and perseverance for the process—and what sustained Paul can sustain you and me as well.

GOD IS AT WORK

The call of God in the lives of believers means that God *has been* at work in them, and the evidences of grace reveal that He *is* at work in the present. And we will motivate others by grace when we perceive where and how He is at work in their lives and humbly let them know.

They need to know because so often they're unaware. Too many Christians are more readily aware of the absence of God than they are of the presence of God, and they are more aware of sin than they are of grace.

God is at work. We motivate others by grace when we help them to see this, and one of the greatest joys we can experience is when we watch them come to that awareness.

For too many, their understanding of God's activity has been reduced to the spectacular, and it appears to them that the spectacular is something that happens only to someone else, never to them. That's why we need to study the broad work of the Spirit so we can recognize His activity in others' lives and can point it out to them. For example, some of the greatest manifestations of power I've seen are in individuals who suffer greatly and yet aren't complaining. That is spiritual *power.* I try to draw their attention to that, helping them understand that this response isn't simply their natural disposition or temperament—it's God's power in action! If He were not at work, no doubt they would be bitter and angry at God in their suffering.

Discovering God at work doesn't mean we deny or dismiss human responsibility. But we're to pursue that responsibility in our own lives—and teach and promote it to others—precisely *because* God is working, just as Paul tells us: "Work out your own salvation with fear and trembling, *for it is God who works in you,* both to will and to work for his good pleasure" (Philippians 2:12–13). This "fear and trembling" embraces the godly attitude of humility; it includes the fear of grieving and offending our holy gracious Father, and the awareness of our ultimate accountability to Him. Our deliberate pursuit of obedience and growth in godliness isn't something we enter into with self-confidence, but as an expression of humble dependence upon the God who is actively working.

THE FAITHFULNESS OF GOD

The second component of the divine perspective is Paul's confidence in the faithfulness of God.

Here was a church that was anything but strong or blameless, yet Paul assures them the Lord "will keep you strong to the end, so that you will be blameless on the day of our Lord Jesus Christ" (1 Corinthians 1:8, NIV). Paul is full of confidence for this church's future.

In my pride, I could never have been that confident about the Corinthians. Knowing how weak they were, and how legitimately blameworthy they were, how could Paul say those things? He could say them only because of the source of his confidence.

Paul's next words are these: "God is faithful, by whom you were called into the fellowship of his Son, Jesus Christ our Lord" (v. 9). This is the same confidence Paul expressed in these words to the church at Philippi: "I am sure of this, that he who began a good work in you will bring it to completion at the day of Jesus Christ" (Philippians 1:6). And in the practice of humility, that's to be the true source of our confidence toward others as well—the faithfulness of God.

IN OUR FAMILIES

Only with an appreciation for the evidences of grace in the lives of others can we ever be truly effective in helping to bring about adjustment and growth—in our families, in our churches, and in the lives of every believer we interact with. Only with this divine perspective can we experience faith for the change, as well as perseverance for the process.

What about your family? What about your husband or wife? In interacting with you, what is your spouse more aware of—evidences of grace you've noticed, or the need for change and growth?

In counseling, when I meet with a couple experiencing unresolved conflict in their marriage, I sometimes start out by asking the husband and wife to identify evidences of grace each has observed in the other's life. If either of them cannot do this, then I've already identified the root problem: One or both are bitter and self-righteous. Their perspective needs adjusting if there's any hope of resolving the existing conflict.

And what about your children? When's the last time you specifically and sincerely informed your child of an evidence of grace that you've observed in his or her life? If it's been longer than a week, it's been too long. You have some work to do and something to look forward to.

If you aren't faithful to encourage, you can be sure you will eventually exasperate your child. But if you are faithful, then when the times for necessary correction come—and they *will* come—the adjustment will be far more effective because the environment you've created isn't correction centered, but grace centered.

IN OUR CHURCHES

And what about the people in your church? Would they tend to view you as just another fault-finder? Or do they know you as someone who actively calls attention to the evidences of God's gracious work in their lives and in the church?

In his commentary on 1 Corinthians, David Prior emphasizes Paul's valuable example for how we view our churches today:

> Paul looks at the Corinthian church as it is in Christ Jesus before he looks at anything else that is true of the church. That disciplined statement of faith is rarely made in local churches; the warts are examined and lamented, but often there's no vision of what God has already done in Christ.[2]

Are you someone who's quick to notice the warts in your church and much slower to catch sight of the work of God?

As a helpful practice when leading small groups and teams in our church, I've often selected an individual present and asked everyone else in the group to identify an evidence of grace they've seen in that person's life. This can be so encouraging because it's amazing how often believers are unaware of the specific progress they're making—even progress that is obvious to everyone else.

THE RIGHT PREOCCUPATION

We mortify pride and cultivate humility by identifying evidences of grace in those around us—evidences that we become aware of only through a divine perspective that recognizes God's active work and calling in their lives and that places full confidence in His faithfulness to complete the work He has begun. Without this perspective, we'll always tend to be critical and pessimistic in our attitude toward others.

Don't misunderstand me on this: It's not that we should dismiss or ignore any need for correction, especially in how parents relate to their children and how church leaders relate to the church. But any correction will not be effective unless you approach it with a divine perspective of those you're correcting, because your heart won't be filled with affection for them or with a fresh faith for change on their behalf. And they'll be sure to sense that lack in your heart.

So let's emulate Paul's humble example and be preoccupied with the divine perspective that makes possible the deepest affection for others, as well as effective service and ministry to them. And in the process, we'll be cultivating authentic humility—a heart more concerned with God's glory than our own, and more intent on serving others than ourselves. This indeed is the posture of humility to which God looks.

Notes

1. Charles Spurgeon, "A Defense of Calvinism," www.spurgeon.org/calvinis.htm (accessed Aug. 3, 2005).
2. David Prior, *The Message of 1 Corinthians: Life in the Local Church* (Downers Grove, IL: InterVarsity Press, 1985), 23.

9

ENCOURAGING OTHERS

W HEN IT COMES to this next item on my list—
Encourage others each and every day—nothing's
more important than our words.

Did you know that, on average, each of us speaks
about twenty-five thousand words daily? My last book
didn't have that many words. A lot of language is flowing
out of our mouths every day and having an impact on
those around us. But how much of that flow is fulfilling
God's intended purpose for our speech? How much of it
reflects pride, rather than a gospel-motivated humility?

WORDS WITH POWER AND PURPOSE

Our words are powerful. Our words *matter.* "Death and life
are in the power of the tongue" (Proverbs 18:21). It's God
Himself who has given this force and significance to our

verbal communication. And He's designed our speech with such power for one primary purpose. Do you know what that purpose is?

In a brief but deeply profound passage, Paul provides a wealth of understanding about our words and their God-ordained goal—both what it is, and what it clearly is not:

> Let no corrupting talk come out of your mouths, but only such as is good for building up, as fits the occasion, that it may give grace to those who hear. (Ephesians 4:29)

Notice how comprehensively this command applies to our speech: "Let *no*...but *only*..." There's a certain kind of speech that's *never* to come from our mouths, and another kind that should be in *everything* we say. That's how extensive the reach of this command really is. Paul employs a contrast here to teach us—this verse is a "not that/but this" statement, clearly showing us the kinds of words God forbids as well as the kinds of words He requires.

WORDS THAT BRING DECAY

The speech that's forbidden is "corrupting talk." Are you familiar with corrupting talk? Sure you are. It's a daily temptation and tendency for all of us.

This word *corrupting* is the same one used to denote the spoiling or decaying of food. Corrupting words bring rottenness; they're death-giving words instead of life-giving words. God in this passage is wisely forbidding us from any and all speech that is detrimental to others—words that defile someone, words that are divisive or degrading.

This takes in negative forms of speech that Paul has already spoken against in this letter, including "falsehood" (Ephesians 4:25), "slander" (4:31), and vulgarity (5:4). But now with the phrase "corrupting talk" he introduces a broader category. He's referring to any and all communication that deters growth in godliness; any speech that hinders the cultivation of godly relationships; any words that have a deadening or dulling effect on the soul of another.

It's the nature of such corrupt words to penetrate and to spread, and they "grieve the Holy Spirit of God" (4:30). Therefore, *no* talk of this kind is allowed. Among believers and their families in the church of Jesus Christ, there's to be *no* decay-spreading communication *of any kind, in any form, at any time, by anyone.*

From God's perspective, how many of your twenty-five thousand words each day could be characterized as corrupting talk?

WORDS THAT BUILD UP

Besides warning us about the wrong kind of speech, God also gives us a positive command in Ephesians 4:29. Our words are intended to communicate encouragement. Our words are to *edify*—they should be "good for building up." And that goes for *all* our speech. We're specifically commanded to communicate "only" that which edifies.

What are edifying words?

Here's what they're not. They're not simply polite words. This verse isn't an exhortation to niceness or social protocol. And it certainly isn't talking about flattery or about superficial words or about compliments that are man-centered or man-exalting.

Truly edifying words are words that reveal the character and the promises and the activity of God. They're cross-centered words. They're words rooted in and derived from Scripture, words that identify the active presence of God, and words that communicate the evidences of grace that you observe in others. They're words that flow from a humble heart.

We're commanded to communicate *only* words like these that are good for building up another. What a sweet command! What a privilege!

Since Scripture informs us that God is at work in every soul that has been truly regenerated, we have this joy of bringing to the attention of every Christian in our relational world how we perceive God to be at work in their lives. We get to enter their lives, discern how God is actively present, draw attention to that, and then celebrate it! And so we leave behind a soul that has been built up and edified.

That's our privilege and also our responsibility, for what's before us here is specifically a command. It's a command to speak words that encourage and edify. But there's more here as well.

APPROPRIATE WORDS

Paul teaches us that encouragement is the effect of *appropriate* words—"as fits the occasion" (v. 29)—appropriate to the person I'm seeking to serve.

To effectively encourage or edify a person I must know something about that individual, which comes through studying that person, asking questions, and carefully listening. That's what we'll do if we're trying to truly serve others with our words and not simply impress them. From what we learn about others, we're able to answer this question: What do *they* need *now*? Is it counsel? Exhortation? Warning? Comfort? Forgiveness? All of the above?

In 1 Thessalonians 5:14, Paul urges us, "Admonish the idle, encourage the fainthearted, help the weak, be patient with them all." So we have to walk carefully here. We must discern: Are they idle? Are they fainthearted? Are they weak? Because it would be unwise for us to admonish the weak, and just as unwise to help those who are idle. So what is their present circumstance? Are they experiencing a test of adversity or a test of prosperity? What season of life are they in? No matter what their situation, there's something we can say to bring them encouragement.

EXHORT EACH OTHER DAILY

We're told in Hebrews 3:12–13, "Take care, brothers, lest there be in any of you an evil, unbelieving heart, leading you to fall away from the living God. But exhort one another every day, as long as it is called 'today,' that none of you may be hardened by the deceitfulness of sin."

Appropriate and timely words that edify will very often include words that exhort, words that help others guard against sin. And we're to speak in this way every day. It's to be continual, not occasional—because sin is active continually, not occasionally.

As we do, we're first and foremost guarding the authority and the primacy of God's Word and the importance of obedience to God's Word. That's a description of biblical accountability. We aren't accountable first and foremost to each other but to God. As we guard each other's hearts from the deceitfulness of sin, we're seeking to guard the importance of God's Word, because we are ultimately accountable to Him. In this context, the practice of guarding each other is clearly a biblical practice. It's a gift from God, a vital means of experiencing His grace for protection from the deceitfulness of sin.

It's also very interpersonal. We're to "exhort one another every day," the Hebrews passage says. This passage is not describing the activity of preaching. I don't want to minimize the importance of preaching or pastoral ministry; preaching and pastoral ministry are not optional, but essential. And if preaching and pastoral ministry are effective, the result will be a church where believers are guarding one another's hearts in a crucial relational interaction and involvement with each other in light of the presence, influence, and deceitfulness of sin. Guarding is *personal*.

In sacred Scripture, God doesn't just simply describe our root problem; He gives us a *practice* for overcoming it. In this passage He's telling us, "As your Father, I want to protect you from the deceitfulness of sin and its hardening effects. So by My grace, I've designed My church and provided this practice of each of you speaking up to guard one another."

We need that help, and we need it every day.

PURPOSEFUL WORDS

Finally, in Ephesians 4:29 Paul commands that our verbal communication always be *purposeful*, and the right purpose is "that it may give grace to those who hear." The biblical purpose for every conversation you have, in every personal interaction, is that the person who hears you will receive grace.

We're all in need of grace. There's no one you know who doesn't need more of it. And God has so composed His church that when we're together in a larger corporate gathering or in a small group or even in casual conversation, we can both receive grace and communicate grace through the exchange of edifying and appropriate words.

Every conversation has this potential. So let us pray, "Lord, help me discern what kind of grace this person needs." For those who are legalistic or feel condemned, we want to bring justifying grace into their souls. To those struggling with a besetting sin, we want to bring sanctifying grace. To those experiencing suffering, we want to bring comforting grace. To those who are just weary, we want to refresh their souls with sustaining grace. The list goes on and on.

Through each and every interaction, however casual, however brief, I want to impart grace through my words, for that's God's purpose in granting us this gift of speech. And in effect we have God's promise in this passage that when our words *are* edifying and appropriate, they *will* give grace.

So we have to ask ourselves: Is this the effect of my speech upon others? Is this their common experience in our conversations? Do they experience grace in and through my words?

WHEN IT COMES TO CORRECTION

This standard is particularly important when it comes to correction. Before I correct someone, I need to prepare for it by asking, *How can this correction give grace?* That doesn't mean that we avoid giving correction or that we trim the truth in correction. But we must prepare to give grace when we correct, and we must give hope in the midst of correction.

How?

Here's how: Never correct without reminding the individual, at some point, of the gospel. Any conversation including correction must also include the gospel, because biblical correction is incomplete apart from the gospel.

Recently I had to correct my son, and because I was already late for a previous commitment I had only a brief moment to do it. Carolyn was there observing, and later she told me there was something unusual about my interaction with my son: "I didn't hear you say anything about the gospel."

She was right. I had brought to my son's attention that he had violated a moral standard without in some way bringing in the gospel and giving him hope. That wasn't appropriate speech for me, in light of Ephesians 4:29; it wasn't acceptable correction.

The fact is, it shouldn't be difficult for me to bring in the gospel when correcting my son, because the one correcting him is the worst sinner he knows; and the one doing the correcting would in no way want to be corrected without somebody giving *him* hope. And hope is always found in the gospel.

EXAMINE YOUR WORDS, DISCOVER YOUR HEART

In correction or in any kind of communication with others, when you examine your words you'll discover your heart. Sinclair Ferguson writes that our use of the tongue "is the hinge on which the door into our souls swings open in order to reveal our spirit. In effect, our words are like so many media people rushing to file their reports on the condition of our soul."[1]

What do *your* words reveal about *your* spirit? What reports are your words filing about the condition of your soul?

As I understand it, corrupt talk is the fruit of pride and the revealer of pride, while edifying words are the fruit of hearts that have been transformed by the gospel and evidence that a heart has been humbled by the gospel. Only the humble are genuinely concerned about edifying and encouraging others.

In my experience, where there's an absence of edifying words there's also normally the presence of pride and of self-righteousness, because those who are proud are too preoccupied with themselves and think too highly of themselves to care about building others up or to be sensitive to their true needs. It's the humble who are perceptive; they're skilled in discerning the work of God in others because they care about others and want to serve others.

So I encourage you to memorize and meditate on Ephesians 4:29 and take it with you into your many conversations day by day. For recommended reading on this topic, the best book I know of is Paul David Tripp's *War of Words*.

Let's experience afresh the transforming power and potential of this command and promise, so that increasingly a higher percentage of our twenty-five thousand words each day are soul-edifying, life-transforming, God-glorifying words of encouragement.

Notes

1. Sinclair Ferguson, "The Power of the Tongue," *Tabletalk,* June 1997, 45.

10

INVITING AND PURSUING CORRECTION

THE PURSUIT OF HUMILITY cannot be a solitary endeavor. That's why the next practice—*Invite and pursue correction*—has a prominent and vital place on my list of ways to mortify pride and cultivate humility. Pride not only destroys; it deceives. Sin in its deceptive power so often blinds us, leaving us unaware of flaws that others notice clearly.

Take for example the man described in this story I came across:

As I sat with my family at a local breakfast establishment, I noticed a finely dressed man at an adjacent table. His Armani suit and stiffly pressed shirt coordinated perfectly with a power tie. His wing-tip shoes sparkled from a recent shine, every hair was in place, including his perfectly groomed moustache.

The man sat alone eating a bagel as he prepared for a meeting. As he reviewed the papers before him, he appeared nervous, glancing frequently at his Rolex watch. It was obvious he had an important meeting ahead.

The man stood up and I watched as he straightened his tie and prepared to leave.

Immediately I noticed a blob of cream cheese attached to his finely groomed moustache. He was about to go into the world, dressed in his finest, with cream cheese on his face.

I thought of the business meeting he was about to attend. Who would tell him? Should I? What if no one did?[1]

Do you think you have a clear idea of where pride is at work in your life? Are you certain you have your act together when it comes to humility? Chances are you're like this finely dressed man—perfectly groomed and confident, but with a large blob of cream cheese on his mustache!

My Own Cream Cheese Moment

Let me tell you about a cream cheese moment in my life, one of many such experiences that have helped convince me that *no* sin is more deceptive than pride.

I'm in an accountability group with men who care for and watch over my soul. In a meeting with these brothers, I was telling them of a specific pattern of sin I had noticed in my life in the past week. I'd become aware of this sin and been convicted about it, and I'd confessed it to God and received His forgiveness. Now I wanted to inform these men about it as well—then move on, because there was another particular issue I was more concerned about and wanted to discuss with them.

But as I described in detail my sin from the previous week, my friends started to ask caring and insightful questions about the root issue behind the sin. I assured them the root issue was obvious: It was pride. I even transitioned into a brief teaching on pride, then let the guys know I wanted to move on to something else I thought was more important and more serious. I'm sure there was mild irritation in my voice.

But the men had more questions. They had observations. And they began to challenge me to look deeper at the pattern of sin I had shown in the previous week.

Again I felt irritation. I assumed I understood that particular sin completely. Why were we spending so much time on something I'd already figured out?

In essence, there was cream cheese all over my face, and I didn't know it. My underlying sin had deceived me. I was blind. I didn't see it and *couldn't* see it. But they saw it clearly.

In my pride, I thought no one understood my heart as well as I did. But Scripture doesn't support such a conclusion. Actually, God's Word tells me, "No, C. J., sin is subtle, sin is deceitful, and sin blinds you. And you need feedback from others in order to understand your heart."

By God's grace, because the men seated around me in that room are true friends who care for me and aren't afraid of me, they persevered. Though I was arrogant—not only in assuming I fully understood my sin and its root issue, but also in my reluctance to explore it more deeply—those men persevered in kindness. And only by their kindness and perseverance, and only by God's grace, did I finally begin to perceive how much my sin had indeed deceived me. I saw that my confidence about fully knowing my soul in this situation, and in assuming I needed no one else's eyes upon it, was actually the height of arrogance.

They were guarding my heart and helping me to see the true extent of my sin. I thought I'd already wiped the cream cheese from my face and it was gone, but they were faithfully telling me, "It's *not* gone; we're staring at it! And we're telling you this because we love you."

HELP FOR OUR BLINDNESS

The harsh reality is that we all have cream cheese on our faces; in fact, whether you're aware of it or not, there's cream cheese on your face right now. Others clearly see it. And you need their help to identify its presence.

In his book *Instruments in the Redeemer's Hands,* Paul David Tripp observes, "My self-perception is as accurate as a carnival mirror." He then adds, "If I am going to see myself clearly, I need you to hold the mirror of God's Word in front of me." He notes that Hebrews 3:12–13 "clearly teaches that personal insight is the product of community" and explains why we cannot obtain this full insight on our own: "Since each of us still has sin remaining in us, we will have pockets of spiritual blindness…. The Bible says that we can be spiritually blind and yet think that we can see quite well."[2]

That's what my friends encountered in me that day— pockets of spiritual blindness. I was blind, but in my arrogance and to my shame I thought I could see quite well. "We even get offended," Tripp adds, "when people act as if they see us better than we see ourselves."[3] That was me exactly.

Without others' help to see myself clearly, I'll listen to my own arguments, believe my own lies, and buy into my own delusions. I'll forget God's warning: "The way of a fool is right in his own eyes, but a wise man listens to advice" (Proverbs 12:15).

JUST BEING TOGETHER ISN'T SUFFICIENT

You may be regularly meeting with others for the purpose of biblical fellowship and accountability, but doing so is insufficient in and of itself. It's vital, but it's not enough. Being a regular part of such a group certainly increases the possibility and the potential for your obedience and application of God's Word, but it doesn't ensure obedience. I know from personal experience that it's possible to attend a meeting where others are confessing their sin, where others are welcoming and responding to correction, and yet fail to follow their example.

I hope you're meeting regularly with others for fellowship and accountability, but please know that for this to be a means of grace and growth in your life, two things are required as an expression of your faith.

First, humbly recognize your need for others. I'm convinced that left to myself, if I'm seeking to grow by myself, I'll only be deficient in discerning sin within, and I'll therefore experience only limited growth in godliness. That's why I need the care and correction of my wife and fellow team members, and why I must *pursue* their care and correction. I need help, and so do you. You can't effectively watch yourself by yourself; you need the discerning eyes of others.

The second requirement for effective small-group fellowship and accountability is that you and I must humbly and aggressively *participate*. Don't assume that by merely attending a group, by merely associating with those who are godly, you're therefore satisfying God and growing in godliness. That is deception.

We must pursue humble and aggressive participation, and that means consistently confessing our sin as well as inviting and welcoming correction from others, particularly when we've come together for that very purpose.

If you're in a small group for fellowship and accountability, are you humbly and aggressively participating or merely observing? Are you actually hoping to *avoid* correction? Do you experience a certain perverse relief when your sin has gone undetected? Are you regularly informing others of your temptations and sins, or do you present to them a carefully edited and flattering version of yourself?

To help you evaluate, let me suggest that you talk to your spouse and to others close to you and ask them questions like these:

Do I confess my sin consistently?

Do I confess specific instances of sin and not just general categories or general references to sin?

Do others find it easy to correct me?

Do others know the areas of temptation in my life at present?

Do they know the most pronounced patterns of sin in my life at present?

Please don't misunderstand me. I'm not assigning infallibility to the observations of others. But do you have faith enough to know that by God's grace He'll give those closest to you important insights into your soul that you don't perceive on your own? Do you have faith that God will use others to reveal to you your soul and your sin?

KNOWLEDGE ISN'T ENOUGH

Another reason we need the help of others is to ensure that we apply the truth we know. Though knowledge of Scripture is essential and not optional, by itself it's never sufficient. As James reminds us, "Be doers of the word, and not hearers only, deceiving yourselves" (James 1:22). Studying biblical humility offers the potential of making serious progress in godliness, a progress that's evident to all and benefits all, but which can also lead to progressive self-deception.

In his commentary on James, Peter Davids writes:

No matter how extensive one's scriptural knowledge, or how amazing one's memory, it is self-
deception if that is all there is. True knowledge is
the prelude to action, and it is the obedience to the
Word that counts in the end.[4]

Mere knowledge of Scripture is not the pinnacle; it's
only the prelude to active obedience, and that's all that
ultimately counts. This truth is present in our Savior's
words: "If you know these things, blessed are you if you *do*
them" (John 13:17).

It's not complicated! Only obedience is sufficient.
Only our grace-motivated obedience and application of
holy Scripture can produce growth in godliness.

THE WAR WITHIN NEVER ENDS

The biblical doctrine of sin reminds us that indwelling sin
remains, and it is active, hostile to grace, and hostile to the
pursuit of godliness. "How often," writes Kris Lundgaard
in *The Enemy Within*, "do you think about the fact that you
carry around in you a deadly companion?"[5]

Paul reminds us of the reality of this deadly inner
opponent:

For the desires of the flesh are *against* the Spirit, and
the desires of the Spirit are *against* the flesh, for these
are *opposed* to each other, to keep you from doing
the things you want to do. (Galatians 5:17)

Clearly this is not a pre-conversion description of the
human heart, but a post-conversion description of the war
within the regenerated heart and life. The daily opposition
of the flesh is something we must *assume* to be at work in
us, particularly as we devote ourselves to growth by grace
in godliness.

John Owen insightfully warns us:

There is no duty we perform for God that sin does
not oppose. And the more spirituality or holiness
there is in what we do, the greater is its enmity to
it. Thus, those who seek the most for God experience the strongest opposition.[6]

As we grow in our desire for God we'll see not a less-
ening of sin's opposition but, if anything, an intensification
of that opposition. Do you expect that increased opposition? Are you aware of it? It's why we are commanded to
watch ourselves closely. We watch our hearts and study
our hearts in the shadow of the cross as a means of pro-
tecting our hearts from the daily presence and opposition

of sin. If you don't watch, you'll inevitably weaken.

As we mature personally, as our families mature, and as our churches mature, we need the doctrine of sin more, not less; and we need to keep growing in rightly understanding and applying this doctrine.

Be assured that this is no less true if you're a pastor or teacher or ministry worker. There's no pastoral privilege in relation to sin. There's no ministry exemption from the opposition of the flesh. There's only a heightened responsibility to oppose sin and to weaken the flesh, as an example to the flock.

WE ALWAYS NEED HELP

John Owen observed that although each of us can display competence in a variety of areas, this is never so in respect to discerning our sin. On our own, you and I will never develop a competency for recognizing our sin. We'll always need help.

Never forget that others see what you do not. Where you're blind to sin, their vision is often twenty-twenty. And by God's grace they can impart clarity to help protect you from the hardening effects of sin. Others can exhort you, encourage you, and correct you. They are a gift from God in your battle against sin. And you never grow out of this need. Never.

And don't be put off when a friend's observations may not be 100 percent accurate. I've found that there's truth to be gleaned at times even from an enemy's critique. Humility doesn't demand mathematical precision from another's input; humility postures itself to receive God's grace from any avenue possible.

So I encourage you to go to others and invite their gaze into your life. Tell them, "I want your caring eyes on my soul. I need your help. Where do you see cream cheese?" And I encourage you as well to go to others to bring *your* observations about *them* to their attention. Do this with the sure knowledge that ultimately we're all being guarded by Another—our Savior Himself. He will indeed guard us and bring His work in us to completion in the day of Jesus Christ.

Notes

1. Attributed to Pastor James R. Needham in a 2004 illustration from www.preachingtoday.com.
2. Paul David Tripp, *Instruments in the Redeemer's Hands* (Phillipsburg, NJ: P&R, 2002), 54.
3. Ibid.
4. Peter H. Davids, *New International Biblical Commentary: James,* vol. 15 (Peabody, MA: Hendrickson, 1989), 41.
5. Kris Lundgaard, *The Enemy Within* (Phillipsburg, NJ: P&R, 1998), 32.
6. John Owen, *Sin and Temptation: The Challenge of Personal Godliness,* ed. Dr. James M. Houston (Minneapolis, MN: Bethany House Publishers, 1996), 18.

11

RESPONDING HUMBLY TO TRIALS

PERHAPS THE TOUGHEST item on my list for most people—the one that hits deepest, seems hardest to hold on to, and most quickly evokes the response "Easier said than done"—is this: *Respond humbly to trials.*

To help us get beyond our difficulty I want to take you, by way of holy Scripture, into the presence of someone for whom life did not make sense, someone whose horizon foretold appalling and dreadful suffering for himself and God's people, and yet who learned a divine perspective on suffering and trials—a perspective that altogether transformed him from a complainer and a questioner into a faith-filled worshiper of God.

INEVITABLE SUFFERING

To help us lay hold of that divine perspective, I invite you to join me in the presence of Habakkuk. I've had the privilege of spending hours with this prophet, and it has indeed been a humbling experience.

I believe we all need to listen intently to Habakkuk so we can emulate his example when our circumstances seem to contradict the character and promises of God. And let me assure you: At some point in your life, you *will* know circumstances that seem to contradict the character and promises of God, if you haven't already. At some moment in your future, life will not make sense.

To differing degrees, suffering is inevitable for all of us. In his book *How Long, O Lord,* D. A. Carson insightfully reminds us, "The truth of the matter is that all we have to do is live long enough and we will suffer." That's the harsh reality.

Carson goes on to say, "We do not give the subject of evil and suffering the thought it deserves until we ourselves are confronted with tragedy."[1] Indeed, we should strive to develop a theology of suffering ahead of time, so we're prepared for suffering and sustained throughout our experience of it. Because the crucial unanswered question is not *whether* we will suffer, but *how we'll respond* when we suffer.

Habakkuk, as someone who has given the subject of evil and suffering much thought, can greatly help us here. He allowed his own outlook to be adjusted so that he no longer lived with false expectations. He was transformed by a divine perspective that prepared him for suffering more severe than anything you and I will likely ever know.

You may, even now, be confronting tragedy. You may, at this moment, be intimately familiar with suffering in a way that I am not. If so, Habakkuk would like to have a word with you, to both comfort and strengthen you. And if you aren't currently suffering, Habakkuk would like to prepare you for the inevitable.

CONFUSED AND COMPLAINING

When we're first introduced to Habakkuk, we hear a godly but confused prophet complaining before God, "O LORD, how long shall I cry for help, and you will not hear?" (Habakkuk 1:2).

He's confused because in looking around at God's people he sees rampant apostasy and disobedience and oppression, which God seems to be tolerating. "Why do you idly look at wrong?" Habakkuk says (1:3). He accuses God of irresponsible idleness while "the wicked surround the righteous" and "justice goes forth perverted" (1:4).

We must remember here that the Holy One was in no way obligated to respond to any complaint from Habakkuk, himself a sinner. But God does respond. He lets Habakkuk know that He has every intention of disciplining His people, but not in a way Habakkuk could have anticipated. As the instrument to punish and to purify His people, God plans to send an invasion force from the Babylonians (Chaldeans)—a proud, ruthless, godless nation.

This is indeed a shock to Habakkuk's theological system. The prophet is horrified. How can a holy God use such an unholy means to discipline His people?

Habakkuk's complaints continue. He asks God, "Why do you idly look at traitors and are silent when the wicked swallows up the man more righteous than he?" (1:13). Again he's accusing God of neglecting to maintain His standards of holiness and righteousness. God's plan appears inconsistent with both His character and His promises.

Once again God responds, and His response is an even greater expression of mercy toward Habakkuk and toward each of us. It's an answer that will transform Habakkuk, a change that will be on full display for us in the rest of this short book, and one that is fully relevant for each of us who has turned from our sins and trusted in the Savior, Jesus Christ.

The first part of God's answer is centered on this statement: "The righteous shall live by his faith" (2:4)—which is good news for all of us. Faith in God is the key to gaining a divine perspective of perplexing and troubling circumstances.

Second, Habakkuk learns from God that the way of the proud ultimately will not prosper, be they Israelite or Babylonian. God's purposes will ultimately prevail and be fulfilled: "For the earth will be filled with the knowledge of the glory of the LORD as the waters cover the sea" (2:14).

God's answer to the prophet then reaches a climax with these awesome words: "The LORD is in his holy temple; let all the earth keep silence before him" (2:20).

This encounter transforms Habakkuk's heart before God. For as the third and final chapter of this brief book begins, the prophet we now see bears no resemblance to the man we saw in chapters 1 and 2. He has been transformed from questioning to praying, from confusion to certainty, from being perplexed to fully trusting in God.

What a surprise! A cataclysmic change has occurred in the disposition of Habakkuk's heart, and yet there has been absolutely no improvement in his circumstances. Nothing has changed, and yet, for Habakkuk's heart, everything has changed. He's no longer proud; his soul is no longer puffed up. Instead he's humbly trusting God. Having been informed by God that the righteous one lives by his faith, Habakkuk has become an illustration and the personification of that truth. *Faith* is indeed what he's now living by.

Three characteristics of his transformation are on particular display in chapter 3, and they represent three prominent marks of anyone who's truly humble before God. Such a person is (1) prayerful before God, (2) waiting on God, and (3) rejoicing in God. Habakkuk shows us all three.

GOD-CENTERED PRAYER

Notice the quick declaration that begins chapter 3: "A prayer of Habakkuk the prophet." Habakkuk is no longer questioning God, but humbly and appropriately praying to God.

And observe the content of his prayer. It isn't focused on his own needs or his confusion or his complaints about evildoers or the Babylonians; rather, it's distinctively and decidedly God-centered. "O LORD, I have heard the report of *you*, and *your* work, O LORD, do I fear" (3:2).

Habakkuk has become preoccupied with God, and now he's passionate about God's activity and purpose in history: "Your work, O LORD, do I fear. In the midst of the years revive it; in the midst of the years make it known" (3:2).

Habakkuk has been assured of suffering. God has made it clear that the Babylonians *will* invade and there's no place to run, no place to hide. Habakkuk, along with all of God's people, *will* suffer. Yet what do we find Habakkuk praying in this same verse? "O LORD…in wrath remember mercy" (3:2). His plea for mercy is centered in a prayer for the fulfillment of God's purposes.

A FOCUS ON SALVATION, NOT SUFFERING

Throughout the rest of Habakkuk's prayer in this chapter, he strengthens his faith through a historical review of the decisive events in the history of Israel's salvation, with an emphasis on the exodus. He acknowledges how God has dealt in history with a succession of Israel's enemies, and states his belief that God will eventually deal with the Babylonians as well. He knows God will act decisively for His people's deliverance—"for the salvation of your people, for the salvation of your anointed" (3:13).

Notice especially the emphatic beginning of this review of God's salvation work: "God came…" (3:3). Habakkuk no longer sees God as being idle in response to His people. No, God *came!* He hasn't been idle in the past, He isn't idle in the present, and He will not be idle in the future.

Isn't this same truth at the heart of our own salvation history, in the person and work of our Savior? *"Christ Jesus came* into the world to save sinners" (1 Timothy 1:15). *"The Son of Man came…*to give his life as a ransom for many" (Matthew 20:28). *"The Son of Man came* to seek and to save the lost" (Luke 19:10).

Listen to your Savior's testimony: "*I came* not to call the righteous, but sinners" (Mark 2:17). "*I came* that they may have life and have it abundantly" (John 10:10). "*I came* from the Father and have come into the world" (John 16:28). "*I have come* into the world as light" (John 12:46). "For this purpose *I have come* into the world—to bear witness to the truth" (John 18:37). "Behold, *I have come* to do your will, O God" (Hebrews 10:7).

God has come to us! Our Savior *came!*

So ask yourself this: When you encounter trial and suffering, what's the content of *your* prayer?

If yours is primarily a plea for relief from suffering, then please know that this *is* biblical. It's certainly not unbiblical. We're encouraged by God in Scripture to pray for relief from suffering (as Paul did in 2 Corinthians 12:8). But this should never be the exclusive focus of our prayers in those times.

WAITING QUIETLY

Habakkuk is a compelling example not only of prayer, but also of patience. He says, "*I will quietly wait* for the day of trouble to come upon people who invade us" (Habakkuk 3:16). God has promised to discipline His people, He has promised to judge the Babylonians, and He has promised to fill the earth with the knowledge of His glory; therefore,

Habakkuk will wait humbly and quietly for the fulfillment of each promise, be it judgment or blessing.

Remember that Habakkuk knew nothing about God's timing on all this. He didn't know the hour or the day, he didn't know the month or even the year—and normally, neither do we. Though we find the promises of God throughout Scripture, they don't come with specific dates and times. Therefore, when our circumstances contradict God's character and promises, we're tempted to supply God with a time frame and demand that He fulfill His promises according to it.

Habakkuk's example is different. He quietly waits—and that takes faith. It takes faith to wait tranquilly for something for which we have a promise from God, but no date.

What promise has gone unfulfilled in your life so far? Marriage? Pregnancy? Healing? A particular promotion or position? Salvation for a loved one? Will you, like Habakkuk, quietly and humbly wait for God's fulfillment of His promise? If Habakkuk can wait quietly for divine action on the grand scale he had in view, then surely you and I can calmly yield to God's timeline in our relatively little lives.

Please don't misunderstand this. Waiting is not resignation; waiting is an *active trust* in God to provide fulfillment in His perfect timing, according to His ultimate purpose of glorifying His Son.

Yes, the righteous person shall live by faith—and that faith requires waiting.

HUMBLY REJOICING

Finally, fasten your eyes and attention on one of the most stunning and remarkable passages in all of Scripture, one that's found at the close of Habakkuk's book:

> Though the fig tree should not blossom,
> nor fruit be on the vines,
> the produce of the olive fail
> and the fields yield no food,
> the flock be cut off from the fold
> and there be no herd in the stalls,
> yet I will rejoice in the LORD;
> I will take joy in the God of my salvation.
> (Habakkuk 3:17–18)

Remember that this is not a mere fading away of some pleasant pastoral scene that Habakkuk is referring to. What's in view for him is the complete destruction of his people's land and livelihood. The circumstances he envisions are appalling and horrific.

The "though" at the beginning of this passage is not

hypothetical; Habakkuk understands keenly the acuteness of suffering that he and his homeland *will* experience when the Babylonians invade. It will mean the loss not only of all luxuries but of all necessities—even to the extent that there is *"no* food." Habakkuk was by no means unaware of the Babylonians' methods as conquerors: They would pillage the entire land and capture and deport the people. There would be indiscriminate violence and destruction. That was the reality Habakkuk faced.

And his response?

"Yet I will rejoice."

Here is truly the full and final resolution of the conflict we first saw raging in the prophet's soul beginning in chapter 1. Habakkuk at last is liberated from superficial, circumstantial happiness. The source and object of his rejoicing is *God Himself:* "I will rejoice *in the* LORD; I will take joy *in the God of my salvation."* Habakkuk has discovered true joy, which transcends circumstances and exists *even in the midst of severe suffering*—a joy found in God alone. And here alone is where you and I can find joy in the midst of our severest suffering.

Without ignoring the reality of suffering, Habakkuk turned his attention away from it and fixed his gaze upon the more serious and critical issue of *salvation.* He turned away from temporary trials to discover joy in "the God of my salvation," the God who delivers him not only from present judgment, but, more important, from future judgment. That's why he can sing.

YOUR RESPONSE IN SUFFERING

So which are you more aware of? Your present suffering or your salvation, this "great salvation" (Hebrews 2:3) that is ours in Jesus Christ?

I admit, you may be intimately familiar with painful suffering to a degree that I personally can't relate to, and if so, you might be saying, "Who are *you* to talk to *me* about suffering?" If that's your attitude, I can understand.

But if that attitude is yours, let me tell you with genuine care and compassion that if you listen carefully to Habakkuk, you can move beyond it and learn to find joy in an unexpected place.

I'm not minimizing your suffering or your pain; if somehow I could spend time with you personally, I think you'd find me empathetic and supportive in your trial. But I would also want to help you with a divine perspective that provides more substantive help and has a more life-transforming effect than is possible through mere empathy. If, in your suffering, you discover the divine perspective Habakkuk experienced, you can know the same cataclysmic change that took place in his heart and life, a change so dramatic it could make you virtually unrecognizable to your friends and family.

Here's what Habakkuk learned: Those who know true joy in the midst of suffering are those who recognize that, in this life, our suffering is never as great or as serious as our sins. As Jonathan Edwards wrote, "How far less [are] the greatest afflictions that we meet with in this world…than we have deserved!"[2] That's a divine perspective of suffering. Regardless of the severity of suffering we experience in this life, it will always be less than what we have deserved for our sins.

So how will we respond when our circumstances seem to contradict God's character and promises? How will we react when God appears to be idle to us, when He seems to be tolerating sin and refusing to relieve suffering? How will we respond when life doesn't make sense?

Will we resemble the Habakkuk of chapters 1 and 2? Or will we be more like the transformed prophet we hear from in chapter 3? Will we be complaining? Or trusting? Will we react to our trials with anger or resentment or indignation—or by asking God to be glorified in and through our suffering?

AN ABSENCE OF ANGER

Before we move on, let me illustrate the transforming effect of a divine perspective with a story from the life of my older sister Sharon.

A few Christmases ago, as our extended family gathered to celebrate, Sharon's husband, Dave, mentioned some physical difficulties he was experiencing, so I gathered family members to pray for him. No one imagined the source or the severity of the symptoms he described; within a week, Dave was diagnosed with a brain tumor.

It was a particularly aggressive tumor, as we all soon learned. After surgery and unsuccessful chemotherapy, it wasn't long before Dave was brought home from the hospital and placed under hospice care to await what now appeared inevitable, and which indeed came quickly. The following July, Dave went to be with the Lord.

During those last few weeks, Dave's bed was set up in the center of their living room, where a parade of caring people visited him. Sharon would often sit beside him and stroke his hair and, whether he was conscious or not, speak into his ear, telling her "bud" what a wonderful, godly husband and father he was.

On one occasion, a relative of Dave was visiting, a man who was not a Christian. As he watched Sharon caring for Dave and thought about Dave's relative youth and the children he would leave behind, anger seemed to well up from within him—anger directed at the God whom Dave and Sharon were professing to believe in.

He asked Sharon, "Why aren't you angry?"

She turned to him and answered with the truth of the gospel: "Dave deserved hell for his sins, just like you and me, and yet God, in His mercy, forgave him because of the life, death, and resurrection of Jesus Christ. Dave is going to heaven," she said. "How could I be angry at God for taking him to heaven?"

It was an answer I'm sure he wasn't expecting, and one that I doubt he'll ever forget.

After Dave's death, Sharon asked me to participate in the memorial service. As is so typical of my sister, she told me, "I want you to preach the gospel." She anticipated a large number of unsaved people attending the service— and preaching the gospel to them, she assured me, is what Dave would want.

But I can tell you, it was one of the hardest things I've ever done. As the service unfolded, I did my best to keep from breaking down as I sat through a video presentation and review of Dave's life, and as I heard his children stand up before this large crowd and honor their father. Then it was my turn to come up to present the gospel, when all I wanted was to sit and cry.

But I forced myself to stand before Dave's friends and family. "You know," I told them, "we like to ignore death;

we don't like to look death in the eye. But we can't turn away today, can we? Death is looking us in the eye—and we've got to look back." I talked to them about God's wrath, and about the Savior receiving that wrath upon Himself so that sinners like you and me could be forgiven. And I invited them to turn from their sins and to trust the Savior.

My sister had profoundly demonstrated the divine perspective in suffering that comes so hard for most of us. In her severe trial, Sharon's preoccupation was not her own suffering, painful and real though it was. Instead, her focus was on the grace of God. That grace, through the Savior, provided salvation for her husband and strength for herself in the midst of suffering, and her concern was for others to hear for themselves the good news of this Savior.

I'M NO EXAMPLE

One of my challenges in communicating on this subject is that I don't consider myself an example of severe suffering. I'm not sure that I have ever suffered significantly. And too often when I experience even a mild trial, I resemble the complaining prophet Habakkuk in chapter 1 much more than I resemble him in chapter 3. Rather than praying and being concerned about God's glory, rather than seeking to discern His purpose, rather than appealing for Him to be glorified in and through my trial, I'm instead questioning and complaining and demanding relief.

So I'm no shining example here. Instead, I'm provoked by Habakkuk's compelling example, and I want to be more like him. If this chapter were about me, I wouldn't be writing it. But it's not about me; it's about Habakkuk, and it's ultimately about our Savior.

Because what's perplexing is not that you and I encounter suffering in this life; what's really perplexing is that *He* suffered in our place. Why did the innocent One suffer for *our* sins? It's unexplainable, but it's ours to receive. The good news is that this same innocent One has indeed been executed for sinners like you and me, and then rose from the dead, thereby resolving the most serious issue and conflict in our lives.

Habakkuk's response by faith to God's salvation anticipates the fuller promise of salvation through Christ that is ours to see and know as historical fact. As D. A. Carson reminds us about Job, another Old Testament figure who encountered great suffering, "In the darkest night of our soul, we have something to hold on to that Job never knew. We know Christ crucified. Christians have learned that when there seems to be no other evidence of God's love, they cannot escape the cross."[3]

We look back to Christ crucified and we can rejoice,

knowing the Lord's strength in the way Habakkuk described it in the book's concluding lines:

> GOD, the Lord, is my strength;
> he makes my feet like the deer's;
> he makes me tread on my high places.
> (Habakkuk 3:19)

Habakkuk had a serious climb ahead of him, and so do we all. We'll face difficult terrain, but those mountains and high places can be transformed into opportunities and occasions to experience God's strength and to persevere ultimately to prevail by grace—as we humbly pray, as we humbly wait, and as we humbly rejoice.

Notes

1. D. A. Carson, *How Long, O Lord?* (Grand Rapids, MI: Baker, 1991), 16, 9.
2. Jonathan Edwards, *The Works of Jonathan Edwards* (New Haven, CT: Yale University Press, 1997), 321.
3. Carson, *How Long,* 191.

12

A LEGACY OF
GREATNESS

YOU MAY HAVE NOTICED that I dedicated this book to my son, Chad. Chad is twelve and he brings his father some serious joy as I observe him loving the Savior, honoring his father and mother, caring for his sisters and nephews, and serving at Covenant Life Church. Like my daughters now married, my son is a delight to my heart and life.

Though Chad is humble in ways I was not at age twelve, he also has pockets of pride in his life. I suppose that was inevitable with me as his father. And after preaching the gospel to my son, nothing has been more important to me than teaching him the importance and promise of humility. Rarely are we together when this isn't a part of our conversation. It's a topical priority for me.

Often when I am with Chad I will think about the future time when I will no longer be with him. Most likely

I will die before he does, and even now as I think about this time of departing and separation, tears form in my eyes and it's difficult to see my computer screen. But I want to prepare Chad for the time when I will no longer be here to have these conversations with him. More important, I want to prepare him for the final day when both of us will stand before the judgment seat of Christ.

PREPARING FOR THAT DAY

As I understand it, parenting is about preparation. Preparation for our children's future and preparation for the fast-approaching final day of judgment. If you are a father or mother, let me ask you: How's the preparation going? What is your plan for preparing your child? What are the content and goals of your preparation? What kind of legacy will you be leaving for your son or daughter? Have you given this much thought? You should.

If humility is to endure in our families and churches, it must be cultivated by parents and pastors and passed on to our families and churches. That's why I feel it is most appropriate for us to consider this topic before our time together is completed.

Remember James and John? It might surprise you to discover that Mom was there as well to ensure that her boys would one day sit at Jesus' right hand and left hand in His glory. Mark doesn't mention Mom in his account, but Matthew tells on her in his Gospel. She didn't just encourage her sons to make this request of the Savior; she came and knelt before Jesus (wouldn't you have loved to be there for this?) and implored Him, "Say that these two sons of mine are to sit, one at your right hand and one at your left, in your kingdom" (Matthew 20:21). She was ambitious for her boys.

OUR AMBITIONS FOR OUR CHILDREN

If you're a parent, I ask you to consider carefully your influence on your children and your responsibility for them. What are your ambitions for them? Almost all parents have ambitions for their children, but how many harbor ambitions for their children that are biblical?

Do your ambitions for your son or daughter include a certain vocation or a certain level of education? Graduation from a certain college? Professional or athletic or artistic recognition? If so, let me ask this: Are any of these ambitions in line with true greatness as defined in Scripture?

And here's a more important question: Are any of your ambitions for your child more important to you than their cultivation of humility and servanthood—the basis for true greatness as biblically defined? Are any of these ambitions more important to you than their learning to serve others for the glory of God? In other words, are you more interested in temporal recognition for your child than you are in his eternal reward?

Ultimately, that's what parenting is mostly about—it's about preparing our children for the final day. All parenting is ultimately a preparation for that day when your child will stand before the judgment seat of Christ and give an account.

BEING AN EXAMPLE FOR OUR CHILDREN

As a fellow sinful parent, let me explore with you what it can mean to adopt true greatness as our ambition for our children. To help your child become truly great in the eyes of God, here are some recommendations—not an exhaustive list, but I hope you find them helpful.

First and foremost, parents are to *be an example of greatness* for their children. Modeling precedes teaching. We cannot teach or train our children if we don't provide a pattern or a model for them to follow. I don't mean being a flawless example; this isn't about perfection. I'm speaking simply of the presence of grace in our lives as regularly demonstrated by serving others to the glory of God.

Effective teaching, in fact, involves explaining to our children what they're already observing in our lives by example. We should never divorce biblical instruction from personal example.

If you want to adopt this ambition for your child—true greatness in the eyes of God—you must begin by examining your own life and asking yourself, *Am I an example to my children of true greatness as defined in Scripture?*

DEFINING TRUE GREATNESS FOR OUR CHILDREN

Second, we must also clearly *define true greatness* for our children. Do your children understand the biblical definition of true greatness as Jesus explains it in Mark 10 and as we see it taught elsewhere in Scripture?

Here's a worthy exercise to engage in: Ask your children to tell you what true greatness means. In this interaction with them, you'll discover whether they have a biblical understanding of greatness, and if they don't, you need to define it for them. You need to teach them that greatness doesn't equal success, or talent, or ability, or power, or applause. It equals servanthood. And it equals humility.

Something else to reflect on: How would your son or daughter answer if another adult were to ask them, "Who do your parents most admire and why?" If you aren't sure of the answer, ask your child this question yourself.

TEACHING OUR CHILDREN TO ADMIRE TRUE GREATNESS

Third, we must *teach our children to discern and admire true greatness.* Here's another question for your children: "Whom do you most admire and why?" Their answer will tell you a lot.

Our culture daily celebrates those who are clearly *not* great in the eyes of God. And to a certain degree our children cannot escape the world's influence. But are they able to see through the hype? Are they able to turn their attention away from these false heroes and to instead admire those who are truly great as biblically defined?

I could point to countless ways in which our culture adulates and glorifies the undeserving—especially in the broad category of entertainment that includes professional actors, athletes, and musical artists. Are your children slowly and subtly being conformed to this world as it relates to their admiration and emulation of these celebrities?

Here's a recommendation: If you're a parent, don't celebrate anything more than you celebrate godly character in your children. I commend and encourage my son for academic achievement or an athletic award, but we break out into real celebration around my house only when there's a demonstration of humility, servanthood, or godly character.

What are you most passionate about for your children? What do you celebrate in your children? When are they the object of your public commendation and celebration? Let's make sure our commendation and celebration are theologically informed. Let's make sure we are highlighting that which really matters in the eyes of God. Let's make sure we reserve true celebration for that which is truly great in the eyes of God.

SPORTS HEROES?

Take athletics, for example. You should know that I love all things athletic. I myself have been active in strenuous athletics all my life, so it's not like I'm some uncoordinated geek who's now seizing an opportunity to display his inner resentment toward people who are athletically superior. That's not what this is about.

Here's what it is about: Nowhere is the word *great* mentioned more often in our culture than in the context of professional sports. If you watch any game this weekend and listen to the announcer's commentary, then like a mantra you'll probably hear the word *great* repeated throughout—great, great, great. Yet it may well be that nowhere in our culture is the *absence* of true greatness more evident than in professional sports. So be careful about cultivating an excessive love for professional or collegiate athletics in your child.

Now, I'm not opposed to professional sports. I'm a longtime fan of the Washington Redskins, and I'm elated that baseball has returned to my hometown in the form of the Washington Nationals. But I like to think I'm a discerning fan. When my children and I have the occasion to observe professional sports together, I try to teach them discernment. I never watch a game passively. (I guess I never do anything passively.) I'm never just observing. Not only do I always have the remote ready to change the channel when a commercial comes on, but when somebody is called "great" for making a tackle on special teams, I try to seize that opportunity to say, "Now, son, is that greatness as biblically defined? Do you think God is particularly impressed by that tackle?"

Did you ever wonder what God thinks as He watches all this celebration of supposed greatness in professional athletics? I can tell you one thing for sure: He's *not* impressed. If anything, He's grieved over the exaggerated celebration.

That doesn't mean it's wrong to cheer—that we should just listlessly stare and say to our kids, "Don't clap!" That's not what I'm saying at all. I cheer and my kids cheer, but I also seek to impart discernment.

HONORING PARENTS

Who do your children most admire? Who would they say is truly great? Who do they speak about most passionately, most often? Who are they most enthusiastic about? An actor or musician? An athlete? A political figure?

Wouldn't a better choice be someone in your church? The local church is filled with truly great people. Every Sunday morning in the local church, true greatness is on full display in those who are faithfully serving others for God's glory. Teach your children to discern and admire true greatness there. Don't just passively attend the Sunday meeting; prepare your children for it and teach them to admire the men and women all around them who are truly great.

After the church service, talk together about the examples of greatness you've seen. That's a good topic for Sunday mealtime conversation—much better than subtle put-downs of the style and substance of the sermon or the worship songs, or critiques of the appearance or behavior of the people who were there.

And there's an even closer location to look for greatness. If I could speak privately to your children, here's what I'd want to tell them. I'd say, "Have you noticed that true greatness is living under the same roof with you? True greatness is right there in the form of your dad and your mom who serve *you*."

I would tell them, "Your parents have served you unselfishly and continuously, and are therefore great in God's eyes. Are they great in *your* eyes? You may admire some star athlete or performer, but that person does *not* rank higher than your parents on God's celebrity list."

I would tell children everywhere that their enthusiasm for their parents should far exceed their enthusiasm for anybody else. There's no one they should admire or respect more. Because I'm sure that for most of them, their parents in different ways are truly great in the eyes of God because they serve others for His glory, not only in their home but in their church as well. That's where true greatness can be found again and again.

The biblical command to honor father and mother is, in essence, a command to recognize true greatness. It's a command with a promise, and it's a wise command, because to honor parents is to recognize true greatness. So children are wise to obey it.

I would also remind your children of this: "In all probability, you'll one day stand before a casket that bears the lifeless body of your father or mother. That day is coming; it's inevitable, inescapable. And you'll know grief that day, as you should—grief is godly, and grief is a gift. But something I do *not* want you to experience that day is regret—regret over having failed to honor them, knowing that now it's too late.

"So listen up and wise up and don't be a fool. Honor true greatness. Honor your father and your mother. Make it your godly ambition that between this moment and that moment when you stand before their lifeless form, you will express your love and appreciation for them in countless creative ways."

And then this question: "Do your parents already know your deep love and respect? Have they actually heard you express it? If not, ask God to forgive you for your arrogance. Examine your heart and receive His forgiveness and change, by grace, right now. Honor your parents—and feel the pleasure of God."

That's what I would say to them. But since I'm not there to do it—if your children need to hear these things, will *you* tell them?

TEACHING OUR CHILDREN TO SERVE

My final suggestion to parents is to intentionally *teach your children to serve*—and whenever possible, serve in the church *with* your child.

Your family's higher purpose is to serve the local church. It's true that one reason the local church exists is to equip your family, but that isn't its ultimate purpose; meanwhile, your family's ultimate purpose *is* to serve in the context of the local church for God's glory. The church is the true family of God, and you have the privilege to serve in the church not only as an adult but also with your child.

So if you aren't already serving in some way in your church, you've got something to attend to and to look forward to. And include your children as soon as possible in serving with you there.

Finally, if you're a parent, be assured that parenting is something God has called you to and that He has personally assigned your children to you both for their good and for your sanctification. They're gifts from God, and they come with all the grace you need to prepare them for their future—and in particular for the day when you'll appear with them before the judgment seat of Christ. What can you do today so on *that* day you and your children will hear the words "Well done"?

A Final Word

MAY I HAVE JUST one final moment with you? I promise it won't take long.

Before we part company, I must remind you again of that which is most important. I must remind you about the Savior.

You see, only One in all of history has ever completely and perfectly obeyed Isaiah 66:2. Only One! Only Him! And He did this on our behalf, as our representative and ultimately as our substitute, dying on the cross for sinners like you and me. Only One. And only Him! Only Jesus Christ was always humble and never proud—and still is, and always will be.

Paul celebrates this unique One when he writes:

Though he was in the form of God, [Christ] did not count equality with God a thing to be grasped, but made himself nothing, taking the form of a servant, being born in the likeness of men. And being found in human form, he humbled himself by becoming obedient to the point of death, even death on a cross. Therefore God has highly exalted him and bestowed on him the name that is above every name, so that at the name of Jesus every knee should bow, in heaven and on earth and under the earth, and every tongue confess that Jesus Christ is Lord, to the glory of God the Father. (Philippians 2:6–11)

Only Him, all for us and for all our sins!

That, my friend, is amazing grace, simply amazing! And because of Him we can know forgiveness of sins and freedom from fear of future wrath. Because He "humbled himself by becoming obedient to the point of death, even death on the cross," we can be reconciled to God and know Him as Father and no longer as Judge—and only because of His perfect humility and perfect sacrifice on the cross for our pride.

So if in reading this book you have been convicted of pride in any form, of failing to humble yourself or failing to glorify God, take time now to flee to the cross. Flee immediately to the cross and receive forgiveness for this sin of pride that God hates.

Confess specifically to the One you have offended. And receive forgiveness from the Father who loves you.

Thank Him that He's given us means and ways to weaken pride and cultivate humility, including confessing our sins and speaking truth to ourselves rather than listening to ourselves.

Tell Him you want to declare war on pride in your life—that you want to declare war on this active, daily tendency toward self-sufficiency, this desire to live independently of Him when in truth we're totally dependent on Him for every breath. Gladly announce and declare your dependence! Make this confession humbly and repeatedly for the rest of your life: "I'm dependent on You. I'm not self-sufficient! And I'm confident in the work of Your Son for me, and in the work of Your Spirit within me."

"He who began a good work in you will bring it to completion at the day of Jesus Christ" (Philippians 1:6). The Lord *has* begun a work in our lives to weaken pride and to strengthen humility! And we want to apply all the means of grace to accelerate this sanctifying process in our hearts and lives so that we might be the ones to whom He looks, so that we might please Him.

Ultimately, there can be no effective expansion of your life's mission and ministry, no fulfillment of the specific purpose He's called you to, apart from the cultivation of humility in your heart and the weakening of pride in your life.

So ask for His protection, so that from this moment you'll give *more* attention, not less, to the presence of pride and the promise of humility, so that whatever maturity is yours will not leave you more vulnerable to pride or to the assumption that your spiritual growth and ministry have somehow been accomplished by your own effort or gifting.

Acknowledge to Him, "Lord, I know how poor my life and ministry are. I know that no accomplishment has come by my own power or gifting, but it has all been by Your amazing grace! You are the One responsible for these glorious changes, and I ascribe all glory to You." In this way, transfer all the glory to Him—and experience the promise and the pleasures of humility.

HOW TO WEAKEN PRIDE AND CULTIVATE HUMILITY

A List of Suggestions

ALWAYS:

1. Reflect on the wonder of the cross of Christ.

AS EACH DAY BEGINS:

2. Begin your day by acknowledging your dependence upon God and your need for God.
3. Begin your day expressing gratefulness to God.
4. Practice the spiritual disciplines—prayer, study of God's Word, worship. Do this consistently each day and at the day's outset, if possible.
5. Seize your commute time to memorize and meditate on Scripture.
6. Cast your cares upon Him, for He cares for you.

AS EACH DAY ENDS:

7. At the end of the day, transfer the glory to God.

8. Before going to sleep, receive this gift of sleep from God and acknowledge His purpose for sleep.

FOR SPECIAL FOCUS:

9. Study the attributes of God.

10. Study the doctrines of grace.

11. Study the doctrine of sin.

12. Play golf as much as possible.

13. Laugh often, and laugh often at yourself.

THROUGHOUT YOUR DAYS AND WEEKS:

14. Identify evidences of grace in others.

15. Encourage and serve others each and every day.

16. Invite and pursue correction.

17. Respond humbly to trials.

SPECIAL THANKS

To DON JACOBSON, for the privilege and opportunity to write this book.

To Doug Gabbert, for his passion for this book and his encouragement in every e-mail exchange.

To Thomas Womack, for first turning my messages into a manuscript so we could begin this book. Your exceptional editorial skills are present on every page. It has been a distinct privilege to write this book with you, my friend, and without your help this book would not exist. Most important, thanks for your example of humility and your desire to serve me.

To Joshua Harris, for his invaluable help in editing the entire book, sharpening the middle section, and providing the opening illustration for the book. I am honored you would write the foreword to this book. You are and always will be my favorite senior pastor.

To Bob Kauflin, Jeff Purswell, Justin Taylor, and Steve Whitacre, for all your time, edits, and encouragement. Thanks for caring about this book and for my soul. I simply cannot thank you men enough.

To all in Covenant Life Church and Sovereign Grace Ministries, for your example of humility and servanthood and your friendship and your support in prayer. It is an indescribable honor and joy to serve the Savior with you.

To Kenneth Maresco, Bob Kauflin, Gary Ricucci, John Loftness, and Grant Layman, for your pastoral care and for the way you exemplify the title and content of this book.

To Nora Earles, who remains the best secretary in the world.

To Steve and Nicole, Brian and Kristin, Mike and Janelle. There is not a day that goes by when I don't receive joy as I observe your love for the gospel, your love as husband and wife, and your love for your children.

To my wife, Carolyn. You are the most compelling example of Isaiah 66:2 that I know of, and apart from the Savior there is no one I love more than you.

See these other titles from
C. J. Mahaney

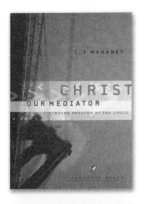

Christ Our Mediator

The key to more passion for Christ? View His death not from your point of view, but God's. That's what this book helps you do in a profound, strategic, life-changing way!

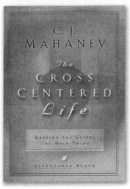

The Cross Centered Life

Does your life lack joy? The symptoms of not keeping the gospel central are easy to spot. Let your soul soak in the truth that first saved you.

BIG CHANGE